Thinking
Visions for Architectural Design

Edited by
Marilyne Andersen
Emmanuel Rey

 PARK BOOKS

Foreword by
Martin Vetterli
Jean-Nicolas Aebischer
Astrid Epiney

Contributions by
Sophie Lufkin
Emilie Nault
Marilyne Andersen
Emmanuel Rey

15	Foreword
17	Facing design complexity by confronting visions for the future
37	Tatiana Bilbao
51	Paula Cadima
61	Lionel Devlieger
73	Herbert Girardet
83	Alistair Guthrie
97	Kengo Kuma
109	Ali Malkawi
117	Edward Ng
129	Susan Parnell
137	Antoine Picon
147	Carlo Ratti
157	Koen Steemers
169	Three success factors for buildings in 2050
185	Re-thinking sustainability
199	References
203	Illustration credits
204	Authors
205	Stakeholders
208	Acknowledgements & Imprint

Foreword

Martin Vetterli
President,
École polytechnique fédérale de Lausanne

Jean-Nicolas Aebischer
Director,
School of Engineering and Architecture of Fribourg

Astrid Epiney
Rector,
University of Fribourg

Resulting from a cooperative project between three Swiss universities—the School of Architecture, Civil and Environmental Engineering (ENAC) at the École polytechnique fédérale de Lausanne (EPFL), the School of Engineering and Architecture of Fribourg (HEIA-FR) and the University of Fribourg (UNIFR)—the *smart living lab* is a research and development centre designed to explore the future of the built environment. The project will be located within an innovative structure at the strategic blueFACTORY site in Fribourg, a brownfield being sustainably redeveloped as part of the Swiss Innovation Park (called "Switzerland Innovation"), and will serve as an emblem of the project's aim to translate academic research into actual buildings.

Edited under the direction of Professors Marilyne Andersen and Emmanuel Rey, who helped define the *smart living lab*'s vision from its inception, a series of books entitled "Towards 2050" will showcase this ambitious undertaking in its various stages. The series notably aims to capitalize on the scientific findings resulting from the interdisciplinary development of the building which will be home to the *smart living lab*. One of the project's goals is to disseminate this knowledge to scientists, decision-makers and practitioners involved in architectural production and constructing the built environment.

This book, entitled "Thinking," the first in the series, presents preliminary research on key issues and opportunities based on prospective visions for sustainable buildings. Understanding the richness and complexity of future concerns for architectural design meant taking a step back from our daily frenzy. Our researchers' approach was built upon interviewing twelve exceptional and committed individuals from various professions, geographies and academic fields.

Capturing the essence of these unpublished interviews with leading experts, the book lays out the myriad challenges and opportunities the project may face, as well as its extraordinary potential to drive change. An introductory essay describes the challenges the sustainability transition raises and which development stakeholders will face over the coming decades. The conclusion highlights key elements for future architectural design endeavours. The book thus offers a rare and valuable synthesis of a number of prospective visions. As such, it can serve as a source of inspiration for research and a tool for raising awareness of the dangers of opting for a short-term vision. It is especially encouraging for those aspiring to improve current sustainability practices, both quantitatively and qualitatively.

We would like to thank Professors Marilyne Andersen and Emmanuel Rey for their unfailing commitment to this meaningful approach, as well as all the contributors and experts involved in the creation of this book. We hope that it may serve as a reference work and a tool for producing interdisciplinary knowledge designed to strengthen both research and operational practices relative to changes in our built environment in the coming decades.

Facing design complexity by confronting visions for the future

Sophie Lufkin
Emilie Nault
Marilyne Andersen
Emmanuel Rey

What will be the role of buildings tomorrow? How will the built environment react to our societies in transformation? Will the design process radically change due to technological advances? Will new architectural languages emerge? This book explores those vast questions, not only as challenges but also as opportunities—from a worldwide, global perspective to more localized, sectoral contexts—in relation to the built environment. The core is a collection of interviews conducted among internationally-renowned experts in various fields that are likely to influence the built environment's evolution. Based on the idea of a transition towards more sustainable lifestyles, their viewpoints transcend the architectural field to address multiple topics, ranging from education, policy and technology, to pollution and social issues related to climate change.

In the same way as the built environment cannot be dissociated from global systemic issues, the future cannot be considered without taking into account a certain historical perspective. Before looking at the multiple futures portrayed through the interviews with a 2050 horizon, we will turn to the past—albeit in a cursory way—to see how we got to where we are today. For most of the topics considered, the full period examined spans 1950–2050, i.e. the scale of a human life and equivalent of three to four generations, starting with the post-war economic boom, which led to a growing awareness of the destructive impact of humankind on its host planet and an unprecedented technological acceleration combined today with a massive development of digitalization. Projecting ourselves into the more distant and, as such, more abstract horizon of 2100, for instance, might have proven difficult, while shortening the time-span would have limited our freedom in terms of envisioning future pathways and proven restrictive in terms of identifying trends in the data that accompany this manuscript.

Global trends

Rapid and major changes have occurred since the 1950s. Concerns over pollution, urban sprawl, overpopulation, poverty and inequality in particular have led to increasing recognition of the importance of sustainability issues since the 1970s, which were notably marked by oil crises.

Starting with demographics, since 1950 the world population has grown by over 200%, from 2.5 to 7.7 billion in 2018 [Figure A]. All three United Nations future scenarios (low, medium and high fertility) expect this trend to more or less continue (United Nations Department of Economic and Social Affairs 2017). Moderate estimates, for instance, show the global population reaching 9.7 billion by 2050. Simultaneously, the population has also become more urban [Figure B] and has aged [Figure C], with increasing dependency of older generations on younger ones. Similar trends are predicted for the decades to come.

In terms of resource consumption, humanity has been in environmental overload since the 1970s. Today, our annual resource

[1] https://www.footprint-network.org/our-work/ecological-footprint/

demands exceed what the planet can actually provide within the same timeframe, and our carbon footprint has risen steadily since 1950 (reaching 1.7 Earths in 2018[1], Figure D). If we continue down this path, we can expect to accumulate an environmental debt of roughly 34 years of planetary production (or approximately 2.4 Earths in 2050)—a bleak future for humanity and for the planet. Although certain sceptics argue against the carbon footprint approach, it remains a good indicator of the need to change our lifestyles in the short and medium terms in order to reach longer-term objectives.

Changes in our primary energy consumption Figure E echo the changes in our carbon footprints, the rise in carbon emissions and, as a result, the increasing atmospheric concentration of CO_2 Figure F. Buildings are major contributors to these global issues: the business-as-usual scenario shows that if current trends continue, by 2050, the building sector alone could be responsible for the total quantity of CO_2 emissions tolerated in the 2°C maximum temperature increase scenario set out in the Paris Agreement (United Nations 2015; Cuchí et al. 2014). Respecting this 2°C goal, CO_2 emissions from the building sector would require a 70% decrease (compared to 2013 levels) by 2050 (International Energy Agency 2013). The challenge appears even more daunting for meeting the 1.5°C limit championed in recent statements by the Intergovernmental Panel on Climate Change (IPCC), which reiterate the critical need for rapid, unprecedented changes in order to avoid dire impacts on ecosystems and human health (IPCC 2018).

Scientists and specialized organizations are speaking out about the magnitude of the threats posed by this environmental crisis. Today, the general public is responding to the call to action, which is increasingly incorporated into public policy statements. What started as a warning about the need to anticipate and prevent has evolved into the scientific identification of specific issues and the acknowledgment of certain observable consequences. Population growth, economic growth and their direct and indirect consequences have clearly put increasing pressure on the environment. Although we now recognize this, it seems we have not figured out how to change this course of events.

Many past predictions—such as those made in 1972 in The Limits to Growth (Meadows et al. 1972)—have, unfortunately, not proven incorrect or unfounded (Turner 2014). Carbon emissions are another telling example: despite many promising international protocols and agreements, the IPCC projections show that annual carbon emissions may more than double by 2050 compared to 1990 levels (IPCC 2001). Another saddening example relates to biodiversity, like Gerald O. Barney's 1993 forecast that by 2015, hundreds of species will disappear every day (Barney 1993). According to the latest Living Planet Report of the World Wide Fund for Nature (WWF 2018), current extinction rates are 100 to 1000 times higher than the background rate, i.e., the standard extinction rate before human

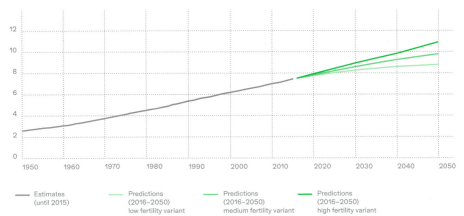

A World population
1950–2050

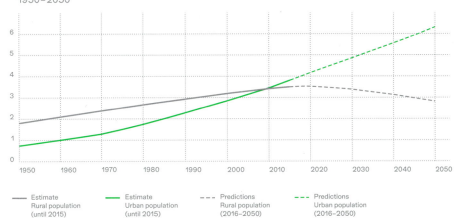

B Urban and rural populations worldwide
1950–2050

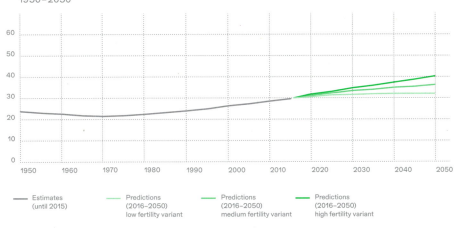

C Median age of total world population
1950–2050

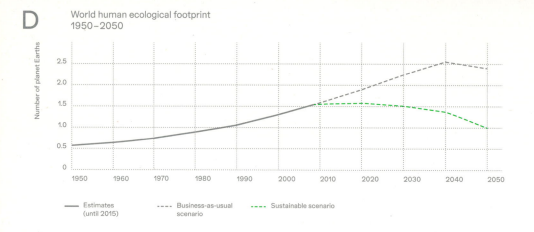

D World human ecological footprint
1950–2050

— Estimates (until 2015)
--- Business-as-usual scenario
--- Sustainable scenario

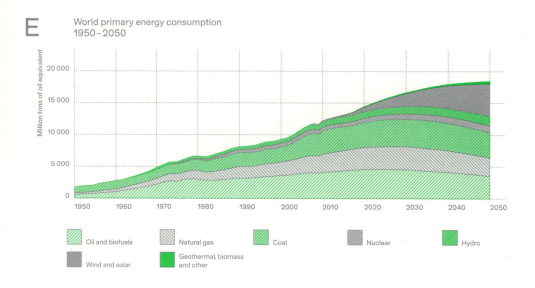

E World primary energy consumption
1950–2050

- Oil and biofuels
- Natural gas
- Coal
- Nuclear
- Hydro
- Wind and solar
- Geothermal, biomass and other

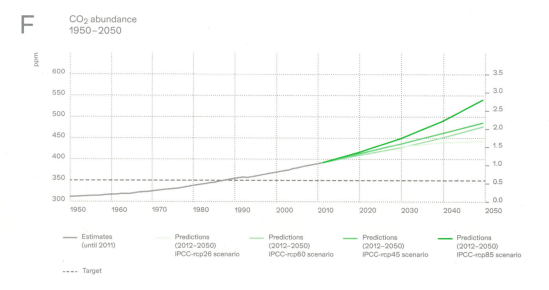

F CO_2 abundance
1950–2050

— Estimates (until 2011)
— Predictions (2012–2050) IPCC-rcp26 scenario
— Predictions (2012–2050) IPCC-rcp60 scenario
— Predictions (2012–2050) IPCC-rcp45 scenario
— Predictions (2012–2050) IPCC-rcp85 scenario
--- Target

pressure became a dominant factor. The Living Planet Index biodiversity indicator shows a decline of 60% in wildlife populations since 1970. For political and/or economic reasons, and due to our inability to plan for global issues in the long term, many of the limits set will most likely continue to be exceeded in the future.

The need for prospective visions
In parallel to these warning messages and despite worsening and multiplying issues, messages encouraging the search for new means of action persist to this day. This proactive perception of the world does not imply that the issues will solve themselves without us taking action. On the contrary, opportunities can only be taken by diverging from the "business-as-usual" path we are on, which means bringing down barriers that prevent fundamental changes by proposing more desirable alternatives.

"Business-as-usual" scenarios and, by analogy, "building-as-usual" projections are unquestionably useful and necessary (in IPCC reports, for instance) as a baseline to compare different scenarios. However, these are not the only future scenarios that can be developed and investigated, nor are they necessarily an accurate forecast of what will happen in the future. Moreover, these empirical or predictive trend analysis and modeling methods are often criticized as being too passive (Gidley 2016): they tend to narrow the future down to what is "probable." However, complementary, more creative approaches with a pluralist view of the multitude of possible futures ("preferred" futures, "alternative" futures and "prospective" futures)—in other words, a "pluralisation" of the future—exist in the field of "Futures Studies" (Helmer-Hirschberg 1967; Gidley 2017).

This book is very much in line with the idea of opening up to multiple futures and, as the title "Visions" suggests, proposes to offer a foresight-oriented, pluralist approach encompassing the wide array of possible directions and perspectives that emerge from twelve interviews.

Turning to experts is the technique *par excellence* when it comes to addressing complex topics involving technological, scientific and social issues (Gidley 2017). The way the interviews were conducted (as described below) is in line with some of the techniques put forward in the pluralist, proactive approach, which include soliciting more creativity, collaboration and transdisciplinarity (Ratcliffe and Krawczyk 2011; Gidley 2017).

To gather rich and diverse viewpoints, we interviewed twelve leading experts from a variety of cultural backgrounds and disciplines—architecture, urban planning, engineering, social sciences, philosophy and history—including both professionals and academics. The interviewees thus represent different continents, cultures, fields of expertise and institutions.

In order not to influence their vision, neither this introductory essay nor its visual representations were shared with the experts

prior to their interviews. However, we presented them with an interview guide (developed based on the visionary objectives of the *smart living lab* project to forecast and attempt to achieve the performance targets of 2050) to help them share their view on the changes that must occur in society and the built environment by 2050. Used during the semi-structured interviews conducted between September 2016 and February 2018, the guide focused on:
1) the built environment as a whole,
2) buildings themselves,
3) experts' personal contributions, and
4) key drivers of change.

Serving as a basis, it was followed loosely and supplemented with spontaneous questions to support a natural flow in the exchanges. As such, the questions in each of the interviews vary according to the specific topics raised during discussions.

During the interviews (which lasted between 45 minutes and 2 hours), each expert was asked to play the role of "prospectivist" or futurist. The recorded interviews were transcribed before being edited and revised. A diligent effort was made to respect the tone, message and intentions of each interviewee, although certain ideas may have been reformulated, reordered or removed in order to create a coherent balance between the oral and written narratives, which are intrinsically different. All of the interviewees were given the opportunity to revise their own interviews prior to the publication of the book.

As you will discover in the following pages, the experts' visions touch upon the different ways through which building design and more generally the built environment can have a positive (vs. negative) impact on the sustainability transition and the obstacles it faces. Changes in the built environment—the frame of reference for this collection of interviews—will play an indisputable and crucial role in global challenges. As energy consumer and polluter, the built environment has a high potential for successfully mitigating the very problems it causes. In a dialectic combining hope for major changes and awareness of the overwhelming complexity of the task at hand, the expert views presented hereafter lay out the myriad challenges and opportunities that design projects will likely face in the coming decades, as well as the field's enormous potential to drive change.

"Architects should design buildings as platforms for people to develop their lives, not as limitations."
Tatiana Bilbao

"Education, awareness, dissemination and research are the key drivers of change."
Paula Cadima

"Obsolescence is 20% physical reality and 80% perception and psychology."
Lionel Devlieger

"We mustn't limit ourselves to buildings' energy performances alone. First and foremost, buildings are places where people want to enjoy life."
Herbert Girardet

"The energy transition is all about electricity because it's really the only energy that can be generated from renewable sources."
Alistair Guthrie

"Sustainability is neither about CO₂ nor about global warming, but rather the relationship to place."
Kengo Kuma

"The field is oversaturated; suddenly everybody's a self-proclaimed sustainability expert."
Ali Malkawi

"Everyday we look at how the stock market goes up or down; we never look at how CO₂ goes up or down."
Edward Ng

"We need to adapt curriculums so as to build responsibility. Do architects study philosophy and ethics?"
Susan Parnell

"Given that buildings are intrinsically linked to the way we live, they have the power to play a significant educational role."
Antoine Picon

"Many people will explore how to create a new register for architectural expression."
Carlo Ratti

"If you try to optimize, you're designing for the average person, and there's nobody who's average."
Koen Steemers

"We should go
back to the idea
of designing
with and
for the people."

Tatiana
Bilbao

Tatiana Bilbao was born in Mexico City in 1972. After completing her architectural studies at the Universidad Iberoamericana, she opened her own multicultural and multidisciplinary firm, Tatiana Bilbao Estudio, in 2004. Her work includes a botanical garden, a master plan and open chapel for a pilgrimage route, a biotechnological centre for an institute of technology, a house built with US$ 8 000 and a funeral home. Bilbao has received numerous awards, including the Kunstpreis Berlin in 2012 and the Global Award for Sustainable Architecture in 2013. She was a visiting professor at the Yale School of Architecture and has taught there, as well as at GSAPP at Columbia University and at the GSD at Harvard more recently.

Interview date and location:
2 March 2018, Mexico City, Lobby of the Hotel NH

How would you define sustainability within the built environment in a 2050 perspective?

TB I've never really liked the word "sustainable" because it's been so overused, but understand that you're referring to what I think it should mean: acting responsibly and not wasting resources. For me, the word "resources" includes everything—social resources, political resources, economic resources, etc.—and not only natural resources. That's precisely my problem with the word sustainable: it is very often interpreted as only the environmental dimension. In my opinion, however, the scope is much wider. Broadening our understanding of sustainability is exactly what should happen in 2050. The built environment should be designed in a sustainable way, but without us having to say it's "sustainable." Energy efficient constructions should be the norm and common practice; we shouldn't need codes, labels or awards to distinguish them. The expression "sustainable built environment" should become redundant.

What are the major challenges for "normalising" a sustainable built environment?

TB Building for the number of people who will be on the planet, definitely! I think the biggest challenge is creating an environment that is both possible and desirable for everybody. Cities are obviously places with the greatest number of opportunities for the greatest number of people. Cities are also thought of as places where everybody wants to live, which is why all the focus is on urban areas. However, I think that if we started focusing on what's happening in the countryside instead—which we, as architects, tend to forget—then we would have better cities for everybody. In other words, professionals should consider the built environment as a whole instead of addressing only city-related issues.

In reality, not everybody wants to live in a city; people have to live in cities, which is very different! Some people want to live in cities. So, let's leave them the cities, instead of bringing to cities people who'd rather stay in the countryside. This is typical in my country. Mexico has one of the highest urbanisation rates in the world ^{Figure A}. I'm just starting to study this phenomenon, but I'd guess that many Mexicans and Latin Americans in general, would rather spend their lives where they were born and where their families live. But due to a lack of opportunities, they are forced to migrate. Their cultural and social roots, however, are fundamental to them: they always keep one foot in their place of origin. So, why don't we work on these small nodes so that people don't have to migrate for economic, climatic or safety-related issues? Then, of course, cities will face fewer problems!

I believe this phenomenon of accelerated urbanisation is one of our major challenges, but it will also be our greatest opportunity on a 2050 horizon. How can we re-root people? How can we tackle hunger, war, unemployment and healthcare to prevent people from having to migrate by necessity? For me, this is a sustainable way to approach the built environment. Currently, many global policies address environmental and climate change issues, but none—or few—target rural areas. Some countries have developed initiatives, but what public policies have been implemented at the global scale to keep people in rural areas? What's happening today is exactly the opposite. Instead of "How can we make rural areas more attractive," the main question is "How can we build our cities to accommodate all these new inhabitants?"

Can architects or buildings help to solve these issues?

TB I think that architecture should play a much bigger role than it does currently. For many years, I've been reflecting on the idea that, for us human beings, the most important thing is being healthy. We need to eat, sleep and take care of our bodies. Once we've fulfilled these primary needs, the second most important thing is finding shelter. As architects, our role should be to provide such shelter. Unfortunately, we've forgotten this basic role. Architects are still relevant for society in general—for representing power, for instance—but fail to serve the people and empower them at a more individual level.

Let me explain. In my opinion, architects should design buildings as platforms for people to develop their lives, not as limitations. Architecture's function is not to impose limits but rather to support and encourage human activities. Let's take the example of housing. Houses are currently designed for stereotypes, for a "fantastic" family model that is practically obsolete, or concerns only maybe 10 % of the urban population. In rural areas, this model is even less meaningful. People don't live the way we plan for! The typical house with two bedrooms, a kitchen in the living space and indoor bathrooms is simply not adapted to the majority of rural lifestyles. By replicating this model, we are restricting people's lifestyles. We mould people from different cultures and with different ways of thinking into a single vision of life. I consider this a serious limitation.

That said, this doesn't mean that a building should be specifically designed for a particular local context. On the contrary, people can adapt more easily when architecture is less imposing or functional, and is more open and flexible… simply beautiful! People can cultivate their personalities, cultures and lifestyles. In a 2050 perspective, I believe that houses should have a flexible form that can adapt to the human need for privacy while maintaining connections with the community. They should be spaces wherein both daily activities and interactions with friends and family are possible.

How do you deal with these challenges in your work?

TB We tried to apply these principles to our social housing project in Mexico, whose prototype we presented at the Chicago Biennial in 2015 ^{Figure B}. In Mexico, social housing is a very important

"Architects should design buildings as platforms for people to develop their lives, not as limitations."

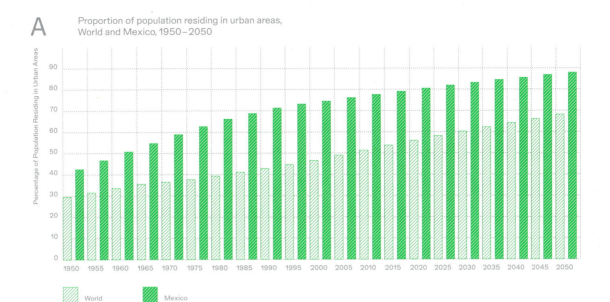

A Proportion of population residing in urban areas, World and Mexico, 1950–2050

B Sustainable Housing, Prototype presented at the Chicago Biennial
Tatiana Bilbao Estudio arch., 2015

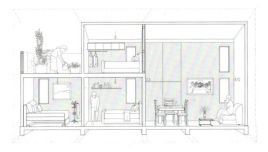

C Summer house Ajijic, Jalostitlán (Mexico)
Tatiana Bilbao Estudio arch., 2010

The project consists of four overlapping squares,
two facing a tree and two facing the landscape

issue: with a total population of approximately 130 million and one of the highest population growth rates in Latin America, the shortage of affordable housing represents a total of 9 million homes.

At first, we started working on the design based on statistics, but soon realized that this was a mistake: statistics are not representative of individuals. So we started visiting people and trying to determine what they really needed and wanted. These *in-situ* interviews and workshops completely changed our mindset. What we saw was entirely different from what the statistics reported and from what is actually being built all around Mexico in terms of social housing.

With this new understanding of people's needs, we developed a project that takes the form of an archetypical house, which can adapt to different geographical, social and cultural configurations. The idea is to build a central concrete core and to supplement and expand it with modules of wood pallets, which are a lighter, cheaper material. This will allow for expansion in the future according to the household's budget, needs and desires, or even local regulations.

Another housing project I'd like to talk about is the summer house we built in Ajijic, on the shores of Lake Chapala in Jalisco, on the outskirts of the city of Guadalajara ^{Figure C}. Unlike the previous project, we were fortunate enough to be in direct contact with the future occupant. So we did this very important job of translating the client's needs into space, which is what we do as architects. We were approached by the client, who asked us to build her ideal week-end home. She described a house with a large living space, huge rooms with double-height ceilings, views on the lake and hills, and an open kitchen. Quite a project, though her budget was very limited. Nevertheless, we decided to meet the challenge instead of turning her away and having her end up with a low-quality house built by a local contractor. We knew it wouldn't be an easy task, so we started thinking about what materials we could use. Wood is not an option in Mexico: it has to be imported, so that was out of the question. Steel was also out of the question because it requires finishing that would increase costs. Brick also fell off the list, as did concrete. The only option left was earth from the site itself. So we tested it, and it worked. As this was the first time we had built with it, we had to learn how to use the material. Only then did we begin the design process, using the material at its optimal capacity. We understood that a geometric, modular structure would be much more efficient than organic forms. So we created four overlapping squares, two facing a tree and two facing the landscape.

These squares are a metaphor for the individual family members, who are also part of a community. By partially touching or overlapping, the cubes create individual, private, semi-public or public spaces, allowing for all possible configurations and relationships of family life.

I think these two projects are good examples of how a building can become a platform to enhance life and not a box to imprison it. I'm convinced that we'll get there on a larger scale one day… but maybe 2050 is too early!

> Why? What are the major obstacles?
> What resources are available?

TB   The major obstacle is financial. Housing has become a commodity, and this represents a major challenge. Offices and other types of buildings have other constraints, but housing should never be a commodity because it serves a purpose, which is to foster and protect life. In my opinion, the major obstacle at this time is global capitalism. Hopefully, society and the people have the power to break the cycles of money and business-oriented dynamics in order to regenerate and humanize spaces. But it's not going to happen by itself; a societal paradigm shift is going to have to take place. People will have to speak up and manifest their needs and desires.

Another key challenge is gravity. In cities, the only way of developing more sustainably is by building up. Hence, translating the city into a vertical structure is a huge challenge for the future. Gravity obviously raises a number of important issues, which, of course, come back to economic considerations. Housing shouldn't be a business, but it must make sense financially. Otherwise, you can't build it.

We developed thinking on these themes with the "(Not) Another Tower" project, a study our studio has been conducting for many years ^{Figure D}. This project is another way to illustrate the idea of architecture being used as a platform (in this case, vertically). Nowadays, skyscrapers—the only vertical typology we have—are extremely limiting when it comes to neighbourhood development. Skyscrapers have become like suburbs in that the city ends in their lobby. Upon entering such buildings, occupants are sucked into a capsule that takes them up into the sky, but there's never any interaction with the city. Skyscrapers effectively enclose their occupants in vertical suburbs. In reaction, with "(Not) Another Tower" we asked ourselves: "How can we connect the space to create vertical communities? How can we reap the benefits of high-rise construction and at the same time strengthen the social fabric?"

Obviously, many challenges remain (e.g. economic efficiency and gravity), as I mentioned before. However, we posited that involving more stakeholders in a high-rise project automatically fosters greater spatial, programmatic or typological diversity. Inspired by urbanisation processes, we imagined a structure that could be sold in parts—not floors, like most corporate buildings—to create a spatial organisation similar to

"Translating the city into a vertical structure is a huge challenge for the future."

D   (Not) Another Tower, Chicago Biennial, 2017
Tatiana Bilbao Estudio with Central de Maquetas, Escobedo Soliz, Fernanda Canales, Javier Sánchez arquitectos, Max Von Werz, mmx, Módulo 11, [raw] studio, Only-if, Practice for Architecture and Urbanism, Rodolfo Díaz, T-O, Solomonoff Architecture Studio and Columbia GSAPP

E Botanical Garden, Culiacán Rosales, Sinaloa (Mexico)
Tatiana Bilbao Estudio arch., 2012

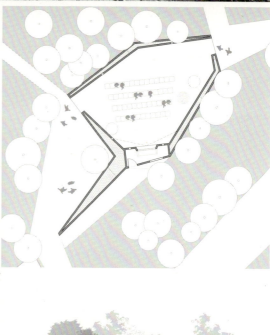

the patchwork pattern of historical cities. Any part of the structure could be sold individually, and owners could simply "plug in" their house, church, hotel, hospital, etc. By subdividing the tower into 192 plots and working with fourteen collaborative neighbours, we automatically create more diversity and more opportunities for encounters, which is what makes cities rich.

The project process was designed like a kind of *cadavre exquis*. First, we invited several architects to develop different parts of the building, which produced the famous image published on the cover of Domus. Then we organized a studio with our architecture students at Colombia University. Finally, we presented the project at the Chicago Biennial in 2017 and at the MARCO exhibition in Monterrey in 2017–2018.

How about the design process? Are there changes to be expected in the future?

TB Yes, I think we should go back to the idea of designing with and for the people. I don't know of any architectural office that doesn't have to start the design process with numbers: square meters, number of units, parking spaces, etc. If we want the building to be a platform to enhance people's lives, it isn't possible to start from numbers because they're only linked to capitalism and business. I don't think this is the way it should be, and this should change in the future if we want buildings to stop being experienced as restrictive places. Of course, buildings have to comply with regulations and economic feasibility, but the design process cannot be limited to these aspects alone.

In my work, I consider each design process as a unique research project that centres on our interactions with the client and users. The built object is truly the result of these rich interactions. I like to consider the design process as a story wherein the main characters are the clients and we, the architects, are just the storytellers. In my opinion, not only is the story as important as the building itself—it is, in fact, the real outcome, just like the building is an outcome.

In this sense, I strongly encourage the idea that users take control and become more active in the design of their living environment. In other words, the character of a place should be defined by its users—individuals or communities—and not by the architect. This is a big challenge for the future. Several of our projects illustrate this approach, but I think the Botanical Garden in Culiacan, Mexico illustrates this best [Figure E].

Culiacan is a city with a bad reputation because it's where many of the drug dealers come from. The goal of this ambitious project, which started thirteen years ago, was to make the botanical garden a reference point for both the local and the international communities, thus positively transforming the city's image. We were asked to exhibit a large collection of works of contemporary art in the garden and to build a series of pavilions and an auditorium. The botanical garden was originally created over thirty-five years ago in a very intuitive, piecemeal way. When we arrived, we discovered that residents of Culiacan really loved the garden and often used it for recreational and/or spontaneous activities. The garden was amazing, very wild, a big challenge for us architects, who always want to organize and plan everything! We created a team of experts (botanists, landscape architects and curators) and studied the garden from several angles, visiting it many times before making our proposal. For me, the most important thing was understanding the place and its uses so that the project could emerge from the place without suppressing the spontaneous life that already existed there, especially in a place like Culiacan. We really changed the way people see art by introducing it in a public space. We created a relationship between the people and art, and thereby created culture within the city. We involved the people in the artistic process and, as a result, transformed the place with incredible speed.

    This people-centered approach to the architectural design process naturally leads to the idea that each building has a personality of its own and is not just a repeat performance of one architect's vision. What buildings and cities—and the built environment in general—express can thus be a direct expression of the world's incredible diversity. So, instead of people saying "everything looks the same" as they do nowadays, I think this diversity, which is absolutely essential, will continue to grow in the future.

    What's your feeling about technology? Will it play an important role in the future?

TB   I like to think of technology as a tool that helps me work in numerous and different ways, and which opens different channels of communication. However, I don't consider technology as a driving force behind design. Technology has an increasingly important role in our lives, though I must admit that I never really think of technology. I think spatially, manually or even in terms of craftsmanship, but I use technology all the time!

    More generally, I believe technology should belong to everybody. Unfortunately, the opposite is true: the more technology advances, the fewer people have access to it. However, I'm quite convinced that it will significantly influence users' behaviour in the future. Generations are changing faster and faster, and this is totally linked to the way we work, live, think and are connected. We should expect many changes between now and 2050. Today, I don't think we're even capable of imagining what's going to happen next. When I was born, I couldn't even imagine that I'd be flying in and out of New York every week, or be constantly connected to the Internet. Social media is definitely changing the way we interact and communicate. It's transforming society and politics. So I'm pretty sure it will profoundly impact the way we design and build.

"It might sound ambitious, but I do think that architecture has the capacity for changing the current situation."

Let me share this little story: a month ago, a client came to my office and asked me to design an office space for his children. But we have absolutely no idea what their future environment will look like! Could we have imagined that companies like Twitter or Facebook would exist twenty years ago? There are so many uncertainties in the future, so many parameters we're unaware of. I don't see how our actions today could have a positive impact on the pressing challenges we've been discussing. In my professional practice, I'm increasingly aware that our role as architects is very limited. Beyond technology-related issues, I think that new professions are needed to recreate the link between thinkers and producers of space, and that this link should be their users. In our social housing project that I was mentioning before, we had the great fortune to go and visit the people and identify their needs directly. However, it isn't always possible to do so. This is precisely where a new profession would be useful in restoring this missing link.

I believe that architectural design could be a tool for changing the current situation. It might sound ambitious, but I do think that architecture has this capacity. If we go back to the idea that human beings need shelter to grow and to develop their lives, then building a house becomes a powerful act! So why not think big like an architect?

"Sustainability isn't only about energy; it's also about quality."

Paula Cadima

Paula Cadima is currently co-director of the MArch and MSc Programme in Sustainable Environmental Design at the Architectural Association (AA) School of Architecture in London. After earning a degree in Architecture from the University of Lisbon, she worked in architectural firms for several years before continuing her education at the AA, where she completed a PhD in Environment and Energy Studies. She then returned to Lisbon, where she opened her own firm and created the first MPhil degree in bioclimatic architecture in Portugal. She returned to the AA following a stay at the European Commission in Brussels.

Interview date and location:
27 February 2017, London, AA

How would you define sustainability in the built environment?

PC   Sustainability is such a broad term. I don't think architecture is sustainable, though we can make it less unsustainable. Every time you build something, it both affects and is being affected by the local environment. A sustainable built environment is one in which buildings and the surrounding outdoor spaces can develop a relationship, a symbiotic exchange. In my opinion, buildings cannot be seen isolated.

A sustainable built environment should also be a built environment that makes people happy and serves their needs with the least impact on the planet. "Impact" relates to everything, including how you build, occupy, use, operate, maintain, refurbish and demolish buildings. I'd also say the more adaptable and flexible a building and its spaces are, the more it will allow the greatest number of people to be happy. Designing a fully automated building won't make everybody happy. Sustainability isn't only about energy; it's also about quality. We have to help people to experience built space and how they can inhabit it in a positive way.

To my mind, sustainability also means being able to adapt to changes in society and people's needs. For instance, while some years ago offices were designed as separate spaces, more and more we are seeing work/living spaces. Nowadays, you can work from home—you don't have to travel to an office space—and network and communicate using new technologies. These are the kinds of proposals our students are coming up with, especially with some cities becoming so unsustainable in terms of mobility. It's also a way of helping address this issue by reducing travel.

What are the challenges and opportunities?

PC   Population growth, cities becoming more populated and more polluted, on the one hand. Mobility on the other hand. I see all of these challenges as opportunities for designers to be more creative and inventive. For instance, in London, which is a huge city, I get the sense that more people are sharing and that spaces are becoming smaller. Doing this without affecting quality is a challenge: how can you encourage people to live in smaller or shared spaces, without losing quality and healthy living?

Pollution is a major problem ^{Figure A}. In my view, a sustainable building should respond to the local climate. If the air is polluted, then it is even more challenging to use natural ventilation. That is why we call for a holistic approach, and not just one that focuses on the building. By changing our cities through design, we can also make them less polluted.

Climate change is another challenge, but I think we already have a lot of research on that subject. We know the climate is changing, and we can learn from warmer cities. The strategies are there, and the technology is evolving.

> "Sustainability means being able to adapt to changes in society and people's needs."

Regarding the existing stock, we have buildings whose structures no longer work or serve today's needs. They can be refurbished, but sometimes there's a threshold beyond which they should be knocked down. We have to evaluate and pre-assess these buildings. I think the challenge is greater when it comes to historic buildings, which have a cultural value but must be adapted to modern life. Buildings will also have to adapt to the ageing of the population, as there will be an increasing number of elderly living in cities who must be integrated. Many older people live alone in big apartments. We should look at how the elderly can be included and not necessarily isolated from young people.

What role can buildings play in light of these challenges?

PC Buildings can produce energy, provide opportunities for food production—for example, on roofs and balconies [Figure B]—offer a work/living environment, be adaptable and flexible, and be made from recyclable, environmentally-friendly materials. I don't claim that a building should last forever. Cities can change, and for that reason the materials they're made from should be reusable.

Can you tell us more about adaptable buildings?

PC If you build a building that doesn't take its occupants and seasonal changes into account and is completely automated, it is less adaptable. It's not just about opening and closing the windows, but also the possibilities in terms of (re)organizing the internal layout. I understand that automation in buildings can be useful, especially when you leave your office and forget to turn off the lights.

However, studies show that people feel happier when they know they can interact with their surroundings—open windows, lower blinds—and thus are more productive [Figure C]. I think it's also good to involve people in this interaction because it teaches them.

Do you think the design process will evolve?

PC I hope so! We want the younger generations to change the approach to the topic. I came here as an experienced architect, but with limited knowledge of environmental design. After my postgraduate studies, my way of designing completely changed. Some students come very inexperienced and ask me, "When you think about architecture, do you think in a sustainable way?" My answer is, "I can no longer dissociate the two. For me, architecture develops in a sustainable way." My way of thinking has absolutely changed. Even if the client doesn't ask about the environmental requirements, they're there.

The gain in knowledge ought to work in tandem with how you can use the tools that are available, which are always evolving and can help us more or less. Here at the Architectural Association, we have weekly workshops to teach students how to use all

A Deaths attributable to ambient air pollution
(age-standardized, per 100 000 population), 2016

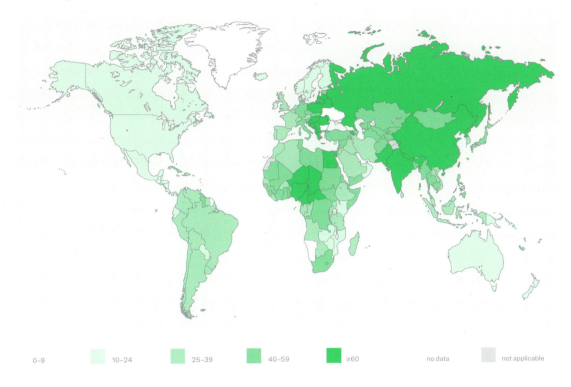

0–9   10–24   25–39   40–59   ≥60   no data   not applicable

B An example of urban agriculture in Tokyo: the City Farm

C Rating distributions for temperature, air quality and acoustics based on the level of personal control of ventilation (left) and for temperature and lighting based of the level of personal control on shadings (right)

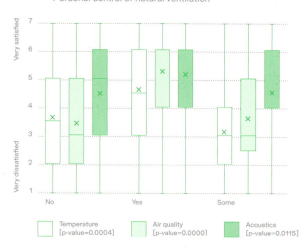
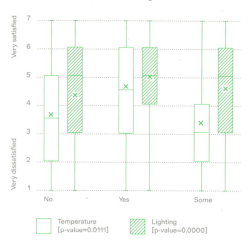

D Example of a high rise building with an active facade: Grosspeter Tower, Basel (Switzerland)
Martin Burckhardt arch., 2018

these simulation tools to assess daylighting, ventilation, wind flow, solar, etc., but we also encourage experimental work.

I do see changes here; some students come with preconceptions about what sustainable architecture is or should be. By the end of their training, I think this has changed.

You briefly mentioned tools. Can you tell us more about the role of technology?

PC   Technology is constantly evolving. The software and tools that can help our decision making during the design process are continuously being refined due to technological developments. But simultaneously, the development of construction technologies and new materials is also contributing to changes in the expression of architecture. I remember when solar panels were very bulky. Now, we have films that can be stuck anywhere ^{Figure D}. I think architecture has explored this potential, but I don't think that's all there is. If you look at vernacular architecture, you'll find that some of those buildings are more sustainable than today's high-tech buildings. I think sustainability in architecture is often hidden or invisible. Conversely, there are buildings that you can immediately see are not sustainable. A tower where all the facades are the same, regardless of the direction, is certainly not sustainable. We know that some people think that just because a building has renewables somewhere, that it is more sustainable than other buildings. Architectural design is one thing, renewables are another.

Materials are changing thanks to technology. Maybe certain materials and their production will become more sustainable. What I'm concerned about is people's belief that a building needs to be high-tech in order to be contemporary and/or sustainable. This is a misconception.

I think it's good to have options. Maybe some people just want to get home, press a button or wave their hand and have everything set to their preferences — the temperature, light, etc. But we need to have options because some people may want this and others may not. Technology should, in this sense, also be adaptable.

What are the key drivers of change?

PC   Education, awareness, dissemination and research. One of the things I see as problematic nowadays is the fact that, because most architectural firms are under so much pressure, they don't invest time in exploring new solutions. What they do for one project they do over and over again because it works. Very often they don't have time to develop new design solutions. It's risky and costs more.

That's why collaboration between architecture and research is so important. I think this collaboration needs to be stronger. Architects should allow us researchers to study and measure their buildings in a fair, transparent way, and be open to criticism. Architects may design something that, according to preliminary

"If you look at vernacular architecture, you'll find that some of those buildings are more sustainable than today's high-tech buildings."

simulations, is expected to perform well, but after it's actually built and used does not perform as expected. There are still gaps. We could bridge these gaps with collaboration: they provide us with the buildings and we study them. Here is where monitoring is very important.

We seek to make future architects aware of these issues as part of our teaching activities. In the "Refurbishing the City" project, for instance, we use London as a laboratory to conduct on-site observations and environmental measurements in selected buildings. This phase is followed by the use of advanced computational tools to investigate the relationship between the building, its occupants and the climate. In doing so, we teach students how to use empirical and analytical investigations to inform design research and architectural practice. Students have to visit the building and interview the occupants, as well as speak to the architects who developed the designs. They ask what the designer's expectations were and determine whether or not these expectations were met based on their measurements and investigations. More recently, as we already have many alumni working in large design firms in London, we have been able to have exchanges with the latter, which are allowing us to study their buildings and more readily giving us access to drawings and technical information. There have been some very interesting collaborations. Very often, after completion of their building study project, students are then invited to present their findings to the design teams.

We also give feedback to software designers. When they have developed a beta version, they can benefit from our students using and testing it in research and design and report the bugs. Though we're talking about tools here, the same is true with design and architecture.

So the architect has some responsibility in this change and transition?

PC   In communicating, yes. I think one of the architect's roles is to be a mediator between the client and experts. We need to know how to communicate with everyone—geographers, sociologists, engineers, builders, etc. It's very important that we know the language.

We teach our students to design more sustainable environments based on the way they think and design. We introduce the key principles, but also to teach them how to use the tools available to them. They should forget their preconceptions. There are certain things that can be predicted based on knowledge and principles, but many other things are less cut and dry. Thus, students should use these tools to test their ideas and refine their designs.

What are the obstacles?

PC   Nowadays, a major obstacle is the desire to have a label, to "tick a box." There are so many labels (LEED, BREEAM, Passivhaus).

Clients want to have a certification label, but some "certified" buildings are worse than others without certification. This is all due to the lobbying industry. I think it's important to explain to clients that just because a building is certified doesn't mean it's better. We teach our students to think beyond that. It's not about ticking a box.

For instance, for the Passivhaus standard, the lobbying industry promotes highly insulating materials, triple glazing and specific technologies. The industry wants to disseminate the same concept across Europe without regard to climatic differences. In some parts of Spain, Portugal or Southern Italy, for instance, heavy insulation isn't necessary and can even be counterproductive in the summer. Nor is there the need for a mechanical heat recovery system. So, it's just a matter of how you design. The same can be said for air conditioning systems. Air conditioning first appeared as a result of economic and political lobbying. As a teacher and designer, I always try to contribute as much as I can. I can't change the world, but I can try and make changes in my areas of expertise, where I can talk to people.

"All the best examples we have of efficient resource use in architecture are from the past."

Lionel Devlieger

An architect by training, Lionel Devlieger is one of the founding partners of Rotor, a collective that explores material flows in industry and construction and promotes the reuse of materials through exhibitions, by developing guidelines and via the on-site dismantling of buildings. He also regularly teaches as a visiting professor, notably at UC Berkeley (2012), TU Delft (2016–2017), Columbia GSAPP (2018) and AA School London (2018–2019).

Interview date and location:
18 December 2017, Anderlecht (Brussels), RotorDC Showroom

What's your definition of a sustainable built environment looking ahead to 2050?

LD   Let me talk about "Behind the Green Door", an exhibition and publication project we did at Rotor in 2013 for the Oslo Architecture Triennale. The goal of the project was to explore the concept of sustainable architecture from an undogmatic perspective. We started by asking ourselves: "What does sustainability mean?" To answer this, we have traced the origins of the concept back to the work of the Brundtland commission. After a yearlong investigation, we identified several layers of contradictions and paradoxes in our present-day definition of sustainability. In fact, we feel the expression "sustainable development" is itself an oxymoron. In the 1950s, 1960s and 1970s, the idea of "development" was very much linked to photography: you've got a negative begging to be developed into a positive. To develop a film, you drown in the right chemicals to reveal what's potentially there. It's a one-time operation, supposed to be applied to everything that could be developed.

    That was the mindset when the West created the concept of a "Third World," that part of the world that is still "under development." I can't help but find it heart-breaking to see Africa and East Asia being "developed" in that sense. Of course, there are many positive changes, but in terms of ecosystem conservation, it's a catastrophe. I think we should just abandon that notion of development altogether. The metaphor has become obsolete and harmful.

    When we talk about the sustainability of the built environment, we must separate sustainability from the idea of development in order to obtain a purer version of sustainability that can be applied to the built environment. We must also imagine the built environment relative to the non-built environment, and the balance between the two. I'd say that the sustainable built environment of the future is one that is as limited as possible and that leaves far more room for "natural" environments. I know that in countries like Belgium, it's very disproportionate; the amount of open space that has been gobbled up by infrastructure, housing and industry is huge. The only little pockets of open space left are, for the most part, used for intensive agriculture. Open space that's interesting from an ecosystemic standpoint is extremely limited. The only future I find interesting when talking about the evolution of sustainable development is reducing the impact of the built environment. It's a question of densifying and limiting our environmental footprint.

Can you tell us how Rotor came about?

LD   We started Rotor in 2005 as a non-profit platform for the study of the materials economy in our societies. Very quickly, we started focusing on the building materials economy. From the beginning, we paid particular attention to the second level of

> "The expression 'sustainable development' is itself an oxymoron."

the Lansink scale: reuse. In the hierarchy of waste management strategies, prevention and reuse come before recycling.

Today, at Rotor, we're active on several fronts. Firstly, we work on a series of design projects—or design assistance projects—where we demonstrate the possibilities offered by designing with reclaimed components. Take the Dekkera Bar, for example, a beer bar and shop we recently built in Forest, a multicultural neighbourhood in Brussels ^{Figure A}. Most of the elements used for the project were high-quality construction elements dismantled from buildings slated for demolition in Brussels. For the countertop, for instance, we used a recycled floor made of end grain mahogany. The sides of the bar are covered with narrow ceramic tiles from Brussels metro stations. For the ceiling, we gave a second life to the light-diffusing *mille-feuille* ceiling dismantled at the Générale de Banque's former headquarters. The new basalt bathroom floor was formerly the facade of an office building.

We are also involved in exhibition projects, such as the Oslo Architecture Triennale mentioned earlier, or the "Deconstruction" exhibition on salvaging and reusing building materials. The purpose of both of these shows was to disseminate our research. We did the "Deconstruction" exhibition in a spectacular, half-deconstructed Art-Deco performance hall in Liège ^{Figure B}.

The research component of our activity has gradually become more prevalent and has led to several publications. In parallel, we also do consultancies for public authorities (mostly from the Brussels region) and for private partners.

To these activities—design, exhibitions, publications and consultancy—we recently added another: dismantling and preparing building components for resale. Our showroom here in Anderlecht ^{Figure C} is where we conduct our contractor activities, for which we developed a new structure—a cooperative that we called RotorDC. However, we still consider ourselves a single organization; the same people work for both entities but the purpose is slightly different.

What are the main challenges relative to the reuse of building components today?

LD   There are so many reasons why you should reuse building components: resource and energy efficiency, pollution mitigation, heritage conservation, opportunities for local employment, etc. However, there are many counter-indications mostly related to how the building industry has evolved up until now, shaped largely by forces that instigate increased consumption cycles. Like in the fashion world, where the notion of fast-fashion emerged about 20 years ago. By selling extremely cheap clothes, shops like Zara and H&M have encouraged people to consume more clothing. It seems we buy twice as many clothes now as we did 30 years ago. Obviously this is the result of a kind of "optimiza-

A — Dekkera Bar, Forest (Belgium)
Rotor arch., 2017

B — Deconstruction – An exhibition on salvaging and reusing building components, Liège (Belgium)
Rotor arch., 2015

tion" of the production process. Optimization here means finding people on the planet willing to produce clothing and ways of obtaining materials for fabrication at very low prices. This is made possible by the globalization of markets.

The same phenomenon is emerging in architecture. Large-scale office buildings being demolished twenty-five years after construction were a rare sight fifty years ago. Today, they're pretty commonplace. This is the consequence of an optimization of the production process (i.e. cheaper materials), but is also linked to the emergence of more sophisticated forms of obsolescence. Obsolescence is 20% physical reality and 80% perception and psychology. The reason you wouldn't wear an H&M shirt you bought five years ago now is the same reason people aren't willing to work in an office that has outdated lighting equipment. Technological obsolescence also induces people to throw away buildings, because they perceive the building's technology as outdated. It's important to be aware of this, especially for the people who are developing technological innovation, which is the case of the *smart living lab* project. Technological innovation can, in 10% of cases, bring real improvement (e.g., the filament LED lamp). However, in many other cases, it's just going to create new forms of obsolescence and increase wastefulness. We have to be careful with regard to claims of innovation. When we look at the reuse of building components and the level of resource efficiency it affords, all the best examples can be found in history. You can look at any culture and any era in history and you'll find plenty of examples of excellent resource efficiency, sometimes on extremely sophisticated scales. In any case, it's still better than what we're doing today. In that sense, we at Rotor are quite prudent about claims of innovation and technological improvement.

We also think we need to work on the psychological perception of things. Allow me to explain by using the example of the "Usus/Usures" project [Figure D]. At the 2010 Venice Architecture Biennale, we did an exhibition for the Belgian pavilion on the perception of traces of wear on contemporary building materials linked to repeated use and the types of emotional responses elicited by these traces of wear. The question was: why do we find traces of use appealing on bronze or oak or natural stone, and not on melamine or OSB panels? I think it's an important question to ask. If we take a more sustainable approach to materials by using the same component repeatedly, even in different buildings if necessary, there will obviously be traces of wear and tear on them. What kind of emotional response do you get to this?

It has to do with how we appreciate things esthetically. In the past decade, we've been very much conditioned to appreciate the glossiness of new plastic, for instance. You know the feeling you get when you unpack a new iPhone, the pleasure this

"Obsolescence is 20% physical reality and 80% perception and psychology."

C Rotor Showroom in Anderlecht (Belgium), 2018

Lionel Devlieger

D Usus/Usures – Belgian pavilion at the 2010 Venice Architecture Biennale, Venice (Italy)
Rotor arch., 2010

carefully masterminded experience is meant to give you. You take off that little anti-static film on your screen and you know that whatever is under it is brand new. This is the experience we have with new products. Plastics are great in this sense because you have something totally unscratched, which is something we've learned to appreciate. Why? Because it signals full ownership: something you will never have to share! Obviously, many industries had a lot to gain by adopting this esthetic. It's something we've learned to project on everything. For instance, we're embarrassed to give a kid a second-hand toy for Christmas. Kids are also very much aware of whether they're receiving a new or a second-hand toy from very early on. To a certain degree, that has become problematic. It's like when the CEO of a company wants to give his employees a gift; he gives them a new building where everything is brand new—from the carpet to the walls to the light fixtures. That's something we'll have to unlearn: our limited idea of appreciation through new consumables.

How can we overcome these challenges?

LD Now we've got a whole bunch of consumer products—your computer's a good example—that are designed to become outdated in a few years. So, for starters, programmed obsolescence should be outlawed. That's obviously the first step governments have to take. But that means handing greater control of industries over to governments. It's a tricky political thing to do, but it must be done.

The lobby of building materials manufacturers is extremely well-organized and powerful, and knows how to push its agenda. Being in Brussels, we see it from close up! European calls for energy efficiency in the built environment are a perfect illustration. Certain businesses—for instance, producers of glass systems, window frames and insulation materials—had everything to gain from the imposition of new, stricter regulations. As a result, because these kinds of laws are in everyone's economic interest, they've passed with no problem. I think it's going to be much harder to truly optimize the use of materials and resources once we limit consumption. We need lobby-free regulators. We also need to create a lobby for the building components reuse sector to counteract other lobbies. That's one of the things we're trying to do here at Rotor, but we don't have the same financial capacity. What we need is somebody who's paid to go to all the expert sessions, and that requires capital. We think it's worth trying at least. For the moment, we know that less than 1% of the materials used in new buildings are reclaimed. That figure isn't extremely encouraging. We'd love to see that number go up. For that to happen, we need government incentives.

Another thing we can do is teach architects principles that will help them design for deconstruction, disassembly or change. We can also encourage architects to include salvaged materials

"That's something we'll have to unlearn: our limited idea of appreciation through new consumables."

in new projects. However, the architect is just one actor, a co-decider. It's mainly the client who needs to be convinced.

There's also a need for benchmarks—for which we perceive a certain willingness—and LEED and BREEAM aren't competent when it comes to setting them. For instance, we're currently involved in the renovation of a large-scale office building from the 1960s in the city center. We agreed with the client that 2 % of all building materials would be reclaimed. It's by pushing these numbers up that a whole local economy of people involved in the dismantling and remanufacturing of building components can be boosted.

Do you think the architect's role will change?

LD   I think architects need to take a step back and move away from the idea that they're unique artists who create sculptures that must absolutely be distinct from the one next to it. The focus on uniqueness and specificity has been over-emphasized and must now be played down a bit. That means letting go of certain ambitions in terms of architectural ego.

I also think architects need to become more interested in building systems again. When I look at architectural magazines from the 1920s and 1930s, I'm amazed by how far-reaching the fusion between building technology and architecture was back then. There could be hangars for airplanes designed by architects, where the engineering solution, architectural solution and system's technology are one, where there's no distinction between the three. I'm shocked by how little interest architects have in industrial systems, for instance. The worlds of architecture and technological/assembly systems must be reunited. Architects should be more involved in and knowledgeable about industrial production processes than they are today.

Of course, today there are more professions involved in building, and things have become more complex. However, I believe this evolution might be artificial. Nowadays, architects often act as coordinators between consultants. That's one way of being a successful architect: be a good coordinator between different experts. In that sense, it's not only architects who have to rethink their profession; it's also important to look at how architects work together with other professions within the building sector. Engineers definitely need to be involved, as do building material producers, the salvaged building components sector, etc.

The changes that have taken place in the built environment since World War II are extremely varied in terms of technologies, standards, esthetic finishes, etc. There's a wide variety of solutions fuelled by demand. It's a real culture, and architecture as a discipline has very much contributed to this diversification of solutions. Young architects are convinced that their buildings respond to totally unique problems completely different from those of their

"Architects should be more involved in and knowledgeable about industrial production processes than they are today."

neighbours on the same plot. I think this is even more prevalent in Belgium than in other countries. We have a culture of individuality, which means reusing components is very difficult. How to design using reclaimed components, which definitely adds constraints on many levels, is a topic that is completely unaddressed by architectural education.

What about technology and innovation?

LD   I think that architecture is essentially an old discipline, and there is no reason to combine it with the idea of innovation. Like I said before, all the best examples we have of efficient resource use in architecture are from the past. What would be innovative in architecture today would be rediscovering some of these past virtues and incorporating them in the way we work today.

"Criticat" magazine ran an edition about innovation in which they cite David Edgerton, author of "The Shock of the Old," which describes the fact that innovation is completely overevaluated in our societies. Even if I don't entirely agree with many of his conclusions, I still found it to be a very interesting read. It's quite typical of the culture we live in today to grossly overevaluate innovation. It makes us realize that when a new technology emerges, it never completely replaces the pre-existing one. For example, much of our energy today is still produced by burning coal and hasn't been replaced by the new technologies. It's important to realize that some technologies are at the forefront, but many will disappear because they weren't made to last. The book teaches you to have respect for those technologies that have stood the test of time. I found it inspiring in that sense.

I think there's also an enormous lack in post-occupancy studies. When we did the "Behind the Green Door" project in 2013, we looked at a number of building projects that claimed to be sustainable. After investigating them, we were completely dumbstruck by the number of claims made by the building industry about how a building will behave once the project is finished. But nobody ever checks these claims afterwards. Our results highlighted that, in the building sector, there is factual sustainability and there is advertised sustainability. Much of what we've seen in recent decades is self-advertised sustainability.

There are a lot of predictions about how a building will behave, but little evaluation of the performances of existing buildings. These analyses are costly, and nobody is willing to pay for them once the building is already built. Yet, such analyses would be useful and would help people in choosing one technology or material over another. Carrying out such analyses, which definitely teach us a lot, would require either a specific commission or could be taught at academic institutions. If even a small percentage of what universities invest in innovation was invested in checking claims regarding innovation and improved sustainability, it would be great… That's another challenge for 2050!

"We need more policies and incentives. The market alone cannot solve the problem."

Herbert Girardet

Herbert Girardet is an international consultant and a visiting professor at a number of universities and, most recently, at the University of the West of England. A former filmmaker and author of thirteen books including "Cities, People, Planet" (2004 and 2008), "A Renewable World" (2009) and "Creating Regenerative Cities" (2014), he has also worked as a consultant to the UNEP and UN-Habitat. In 2004, he co-founded the World Future Council, a foundation that works towards spreading "future-ready" policy solutions worldwide. He is also a full member of the Club of Rome.

Interview date and location:
7 September 2016, Shanghai, Urban Transitions Global Summit

What's your position on sustainability?

HG "Sustain" is a very passive term. We live on a profoundly damaged planet. Sustaining it in this depleted state is no longer good enough. The relationship between the way we live in our human settlements and the world beyond must become much more pro-active.

"Sustainable" is a term that is both corrupted and grossly overused. There are many other terms available to define the way we should manage our cities—such as liveable, resilient, smart, intelligent and responsible, for instance. I prefer to use the term "regenerative." Regenerative cities are environmentally-enhancing, restorative urban systems that maintain a responsible relationship with the natural resources on which they depend. They are not only energy-efficient and low carbon, but also designed to have positive impacts on their local and regional ecosystems.

What are the major challenges when it comes to achieving a regenerative built environment?

HG Cities tend to think that they can declare "independence from nature," which is a rather catastrophic way of thinking. Cities are, in fact, dependent systems that rely upon ecosystem services somewhere out there. It's not good enough to simply look at a city in terms of its morphology as planners tend to do; we need to take a closer look at the linkages—pipes and cables connecting the city to the wider hinterland, the power stations, and food and water sources.

19th century German economist Johann Heinrich von Thünen showed that in the absence of major road, canal or river transport systems, cities had to ensure steady food and timber supplies from close by (Heinrich von Thünen 1966). They had to give back in order to survive. There had to be a give and take between human settlements and their hinterlands. I refer to this traditional type of human settlement as "Agropolis."

We don't live in the "Agropolis" anymore; we live in "Petropolis," the city powered by fossil fuels from global sources. It all started with the Industrial Revolution. Today, with access to resources across the planet—at least in the Global North—we take but don't give back very much. That is one of the most critical issues in an urbanizing world. We need to understand that we must look beyond physical structures towards processes found in natural ecosystems and replace our current, inefficient linear system of resource extraction and waste disposal with a resource-efficient circular urban metabolism.

A massive daily injection of stored sunlight in the form of coal, oil and gas is the primary condition for making contemporary urban systems possible. This is the key issue we now have to deal with. Of course, individual consumers cannot be expected to spearhead modern, eco-friendly, responsible lifestyles. In order to spark the significant changes that are needed in the energy

"Today, with access to resources across the planet, we take but don't give back very much."

and resource performance of our cities, we will require national policies that go beyond existing perspectives.

New technical options do exist and must be driven by policy, particularly when it comes to wind and solar power and energy storage. Yet, even with increasingly-popular and ever cheaper novel energy technologies that are now becoming available, we still won't be able to lower atmospheric carbon concentrations. We can only do that by finding ways to sequester carbon, preferably by natural means like reforestation and carbon storage in soils. Yet, in many places, forests are burning or dying due to climate stress and disease-related issues. This is a very worrying development.

The challenge we now face is that of turning our cities into ecologically and economically-restorative systems. In my view, we need to move into a new kind of city, which I call "Ecopolis." There are many cities around the world that could be made to run on efficient, renewable energy systems and be actively reconnected to their local hinterland. Some cities have already moved in this direction. In this context, "energy democracy" is an interesting issue: no longer relying on mega power station monopolies but implementing a much more democratic "prosumer" approach wherein consumers can also become energy producers.

How do you envision the role of buildings between now and 2050?

HG From World War II onwards, fossil fuel energy was so freely available that people didn't worry much about building design and its relationship to energy and the larger environment. That has obviously become a major challenge, mainly due to concerns about climate change.

Optimizing the energy performances of buildings is becoming a critical issue. Passive and solar design are now becoming mainstream, and technology has improved a great deal, with tremendous innovation in insulation materials and solar technology. Thus, a great many new options have suddenly become available and are directly relevant to the future of not only individual building construction, but the design of entire cities.

Energy self-sufficient buildings or energy+ buildings are no longer just a theory; they're a reality. However, we mustn't limit ourselves to buildings' energy performances alone. First and foremost, buildings are places where people want to enjoy life. So how architecture responds to that is another big issue.

I think there is also renewed interest in community gardens, which were both popular and a necessity in the 19th century in Germany, the United Kingdom and other countries. Back then, people—who often had migrated from villages to urban areas—wanted to keep growing some of their own food for their families. I believe intra- and peri-urban farming and gardening is essential for the future of urban food supplies. Emerging technology-

A Cité maraîchère, Romainville (France)
ilimelgo arch., 2019

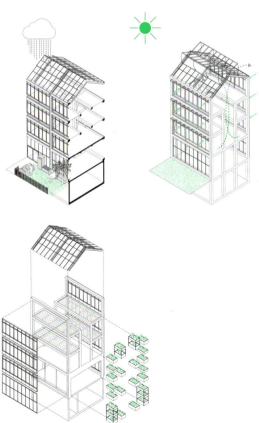

driven options also undoubtedly provide relevant tools, like vertical farming [Figure A], which can be done in old factory buildings and does not necessarily require purpose-built greenhouses.

What are the major obstacles to achieving energy-efficient or active buildings?

HG   Taking the example of the BedZED[2] project [Figure B], the first of its kind in Britain, cost overruns were a significant issue, partly because it introduced new features that had to be specially designed for the project. Generally speaking, initial investments for high-performance projects pose problems, even if operating costs are lower and the project will be cost-effective in the long run. However, Passivhaus design is quickly becoming cost-competitive with conventional design. Still, we need more policies and incentives. The market alone cannot solve the problem.

Can you give us some examples of your own work that have contributed to the field?

HG   In 2013, I was invited to be a "Thinker in Residence" in Adelaide, Australia. The goal was to come up with proposals for improving the efficiency of an energy/resource-intensive city region of some 1.3 million people and, crucially, to help create a substantial new green economy. Over a very intense 10-week period I held daily seminars and lectures with people from all sectors of society. I came up with a 32-point plan, 31 of which were implemented within a few months[3]. These included measures for energy-efficient retrofitting of buildings, large-scale tree planting, water security measures, sustainable transport policies, 100 % organic waste recycling and support for peri-urban agriculture. Subsequently, feed-in tariffs for renewable energy were added and Adelaide now has over 50 % electricity supplies from wind and solar technology. Ultimately, we were able to achieve a remarkable, regenerative urban transformation, moving actively towards creating a circular metabolism whilst creating thousands of new green jobs.

More recently, I was also involved in a project called Dongtan Eco-City on Chongming Island, in the Yangtze delta. The Shanghai city government wanted to build a city that would not pollute the island, which is largely farmland and home to a bird sanctuary. The plan was to build an eco-city for half a million people by 2030. I was working as a consultant for Arup[4], the multinational engineering firm. The idea was to design a car-free Ecopolis that would be largely powered by renewable energy, where waste water would be recycled and reused for irrigation, and that would have a circular metabolism. The Ecopolis was to be built on farmland, yet without reducing the total amount of produce grown on that land. Unfortunately, the project did not come to fruition for political reasons.

2   BedZED is a large-scale, mixed-used sustainable community located south of London whose construction was completed in 2002 (www.bioregional.com/bedzed/).

3   The report is available at http://www.infosperber.ch/data/attachements/Girardet_Report.pdf.

4   See the interview with Alistair Guthrie, Global Sustainable Buildings Design Leader at Arup.

B BedZED, Sutton (United Kingdom)
Bill Dunster arch., 2001

BUILDING PHYSICS

- EXPOSED THERMAL MASS
- IN SUMMER - PRODUCES COOLING
- IN WINTER - STORES PASSIVE HEAT GAINS UNTIL NEEDED

HIGHLY INSULATED = $0.1 W/m^2k$
WINDOWS = TRIPLE GLAZED
AIRTIGHTNESS = 2 AC/HR @ 50Pa
SUN SPACE = DOUBLE GLAZED TO ROOM & TO OUTSIDE

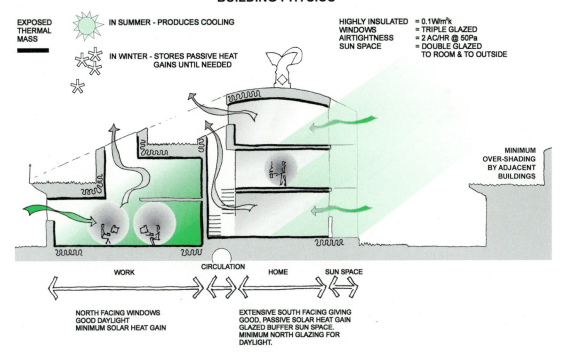

MINIMUM OVER-SHADING BY ADJACENT BUILDINGS

WORK — CIRCULATION — HOME — SUN SPACE

NORTH FACING WINDOWS
GOOD DAYLIGHT
MINIMUM SOLAR HEAT GAIN

EXTENSIVE SOUTH FACING GIVING GOOD, PASSIVE SOLAR HEAT GAIN
GLAZED BUFFER SUN SPACE.
MINIMUM NORTH GLAZING FOR DAYLIGHT.

Herbert Girardet

C   Wattle Point Wind Farm
Yorke Peninsula, South Australia, 2007

D   Dongtan Eco-City, Shanghai (China)
Arup, 2008

Who are the key initiators of change? Are new professions to emerge or roles to evolve?

HG   Back in the United Kingdom, I was involved in introducing feed-in tariffs for renewable energy. That had a dramatic effect on the uptake of renewable energy—especially solar—at the local level. This experience highlights the importance of appropriate national policies, which I believe are key to creating a world of regenerative cities. The market itself is lazy! It doesn't want to innovate unless it's for profit and, by itself, is not fit to create truly liveable and environmentally compatible cities.

At the other end of the scale are citizens. Environmentally-conscious behavior patterns are still difficult to instil in people, but we're slowly getting there. We are now "amplified" by technology—I use the term "amplified man"—with our reliance on ever more technologies and gadgets. Although many devices have become ever smaller and more energy-efficient, we use more of them than ever before—cars, washing machines, cell phones, industrial robots, etc. Greater awareness of our impacts is badly needed. Informing users of the full impact of our lifestyles is a key driver of change.

In terms of professions, I believe the role of engineers is becoming more important. Civil engineering is evolving and taking a growing interest in ecology and the metabolism of cities. All major engineering firms like Arup, for instance, now have ecology departments. The latter are still smaller than other departments, like structural engineering, but they're growing rapidly. The whole environmental consultancy field has grown a great deal in recent years. When I first started out, it was hard to make a living. Nowadays, you see ads for ecological and environmental engineering positions everywhere. These are encouraging signs. Still, change can be further aided by appropriate policies.

A crucial driver for making an energy and regenerative development turnaround happen is to realize that there is huge economic potential in these sectors. This became very evident in my work in Adelaide. A lot of cities have suffered from job losses due to automation, industrial relocation, etc. But energy can be supplied more locally and recycling can become an integral part of the functioning of urban systems, meaning that jobs can come back to the urban arena. But, again, that is something that won't happen automatically—it has to be driven by both national- and community-level enabling policies.

"Informing users of the full impact of our lifestyles is another key driver of change."

"Technology is hugely important, but I don't think it will solve everything."

Alistair Guthrie

Alistair Guthrie has been working as a mechanical, building physics and sustainability engineer for nearly forty years, thirty-five of which have been at Arup, where he is an Arup Fellow and a Consultant in building design, concentrating on sustainable solutions. He has worked internationally on a variety of projects including high-rise buildings, airports and numerous art projects.

Interview date and location:
28 February 2017, London, Arup

> What's your definition of a sustainable built environment looking ahead to 2050?

AG I'm not sure there's such thing as a simple definition. I think the best definition of sustainability is the Brundtland definition, and I don't think that it will change for 2050.

When we started thinking about the idea of a sustainable built environment ten years ago, it was based on the principle of backcasting, which means setting a goal and working backwards to see how you can achieve it. In a certain sense, this approach is the complete opposite of assessment methods like LEED and BREEAM. The latter are good incentives, but you have to start by assessing or building up your project goals, whereas backcasting looks ahead and sets a more far-reaching goal to work towards.

The goal we're setting for ourselves as regards the built environment is achieving carbon-neutrality for our projects. This includes creating circular economy solutions—albeit a buzzword—which means that everything used stays in circulation rather than becoming waste. I think this is a very important goal.

To my mind, that's the most challenging issue today: how can we reduce and eliminate our use of extractive materials including, of course, fossil fuel energy. Moving towards that next big goal can lead to a truly sustainable future because it means that our use of the earth's resources will no longer be one-way. It's a recycle-repurpose approach, which is obviously sustainable because we're not taking anything away; we're using what we have. In a way, that's the ultimate definition of sustainability because it leaves the earth the same way we found it for the next generation. The definition of sustainability hasn't changed, but maybe we're doing a better job of living up to it.

> What are the challenges and opportunities in terms of reaching that goal?

AG We have to look beyond individual buildings. We should consider communities, cities and the overall use of materials within a much larger environment. Working on a small-cycle basis doesn't really work. We need to look at a bigger cycle.

Looking at new materials and repurposing existing materials is also quite interesting. There's a lot of work to be done in this area. Here at Arup, for instance, we do a lot of projects with wooden structures that focus on rethinking the way we use wood. The Believe in Better Building—the tallest commercial timber structure in the UK—is a good illustration [Figure A]. We need to find new ways of using existing materials, for example zero-cement concrete so that the concrete can be crushed and reused [Figure B].

Apart from that, I think one of the biggest challenges for our cities—one that really hasn't been addressed—is pollution. I think doing so will force us to see transport and lifestyles differently.

> "The definition of sustainability hasn't changed, but maybe we're doing a better job of living up to it."

What will buildings' role be?

AG   We need buildings to live in. I don't think that will fundamentally change. Maybe we'll refocus on how we build, what we build and the size of the space we think we need to live and work in. I'm seeing a bit of change in that respect, even in London. For example, the number of people living in apartments versus houses has really grown, mostly due to costs but also because people are now willing to live in apartments. This changes the way we look at our cities because it changes transportation patterns, energy patterns, food distribution patterns, etc. In other words, the more concentrated the city is, the greater the benefits are in terms of transportation, energy and air quality.

That said, we all have to live in buildings, but we don't all have to work in buildings. I think there will be a shift in this idea of "going to work." Huge changes are already taking place in certain parts of the world: for instance, there are certain industries in which people often work from home. I suspect the idea of having a certain required surface area per employee is something that's already becoming obsolete and will become more so in the future.

In this sense, I think people will become more conscious of their living and working spaces. The whole concept of wellness is becoming increasingly important. People want to be in places where they feel they can live better all the time, wherever they are merging the differences between home and work. That's a sort of counter-challenge to some of the other issues we've talked about because sometimes these things work against each other.

What about technology?

AG   I think technology is hugely important, but I don't think it will solve everything. If you look back a little, some technology has revolutionized the energy debate. Look at LED lighting, for instance, which of course required legislation to make it ubiquitous. However, the technology had to exist first. The result is that we've probably quartered the amount of energy used for lighting in an average building.

In terms of technology, two areas are going to make a big difference as far as energy is concerned. First, electric transport, which will happen for several reasons and will likely be accelerated by the pollution debate more so than the energy debate. The driver for that particular transition is battery technology, which has changed considerably. Even my three-year old electric car is now outdated because of its battery. Battery technology is really going to change the way we live, not just the way we move. We'll start having storage capacity in our own houses and buildings, which will allow us to generate renewable power more efficiently. The energy transition is all about electricity because it's really the only energy that can be generated from renewable sources.

"The energy transition is all about electricity because it's really the only energy that can be generated from renewable sources."

A   Believe in Better Building, Isleworth (United Kingdom)
Arup Associates arch., 2014

B   Global Change Institute (University of Queensland), Brisbane (Australia)
Hassell arch., 2013

C Stavros Niarchos Foundation Cultural Centre, Athens (Greece)
Renzo Piano Building Workshop arch., 2016

D Valetta City Gate, Valetta (Malta)
Renzo Piano Building Workshop arch., 2015

Individuals will be able to generate, store and use electricity twenty-four hours a day and not only during daylight hours, which is how things are at the moment. Any excess will get fed back into the grid like it does now, but there will be less feedback into the grid because there will be more use on site. These technologies will change the way we design our buildings and cities, and that's one of the technology drivers that will make a difference.

For example, in London, people don't open the windows in their office buildings — we can't even open these windows here today! There are two main reasons for this: for one, it's too polluted outside; secondly, it's too noisy. Electric transport, which is both pollution-free and quiet, can potentially change the way we design our cities and buildings. Infrastructure — the way cities are organized — will interact with buildings, and technology will make that possible.

Will new digital tools transform the design process?

AG   Digital tools certainly make the process quicker. You can have more iteration and more exploration in a shorter timeframe. Whether they'll lead to more sustainable outcomes, I really don't know. I'm not sure that technology in itself will do that; it won't make decisions for us. However, it might facilitate applying information early on, for example, to help in making better decisions. Working together as a design team with better technology can help, but I don't think that's going to make all the difference.

I've always been an advocate of working in an integrated way and have always tried to do so. In my opinion, all the best, most sustainable projects are the result of collaboration between different experts. They don't come from a single person vested with the responsibility of sustainability; they involve the entire design team, which takes on the challenge together. A lot of it comes from the team members having a clear understanding of the sustainability drivers for the project and not just leaving it up to one person. At Arup, I'd say we've tried to avoid that. We've always tried to work with people who really understand the strategies and attempt to apply them. Integrated design and a solid, growing understanding of sustainability principles is essential! I think technology helps, but it's not a "special" driver or a prerequisite. You need that commitment together as a design team to do something better. Then, perhaps, technology can be used to support the design process.

Can you illustrate this approach with concrete projects?

AG   With pleasure. I'm thinking of two projects with Renzo Piano that opened last year. First, the Stavros Niarchos Foundation Cultural Center (SNFCC) in Athens, which is a library and opera house ^{Figure C}. That project was mainly about technology. What was interesting was that, at the very first workshop with the client, I said to them, "In Athens, the one thing you have more of than any-

"Integrated design and a solid, growing understanding of sustainability principles is essential!"

thing else is sunshine. We need to capitalize on that for this project." I took the site plan and put a square on it and said, "If you had that much photovoltaic, we could generate all the electricity you'd need for the project." We put that on the table right from day one. The project has a 100 m × 100 m solar array on the roof, which is actually about a quarter of the size of the square I initially drew. We didn't achieve what we put forth at the beginning, but it's still an accomplishment. The second thing we discussed was what they don't have much of in Athens, which is water. So we developed a strategy to use, recycle and reuse ground water from the beginning. The project got LEED platinum certification.

The other project is the new parliament building in Malta _{Figure D}. In our early discussions, we determined that the building should be made of a local stone. Every building in Malta is made of the same stone—the island is a rock. The stone blocks were carved in such a way as to shade the windows for much of the building's operating hours. The windows can all be opened because there's a nice sea breeze. We used the building's mass and natural ventilation to lower its energy consumption and then introduced ground heat exchange technology to minimise cooling energy. Using heat pumps, we store the heat removed from the building in the summer in the ground to use in the winter. There's no additional heating in the building during the cold season, which is quite short. This reduces the load enormously, but there is still a small solar array on the roof that can provide 60 % of the annual electricity needs.

What's more, there's no natural water storage in Malta. For the last 1000 years, people have lived by collecting rainwater. They've cut systems into the rocks beneath their houses and have storage tanks. Incidentally, when we were digging the foundations, we found a large system that nobody knew about and reused that as well. We collect all the rainwater from the site and its surroundings and store it in tanks in the building. This water is used for non-potable purposes (irrigation, etc.).

Our client gave us no specific requirements for the project. They wanted a good, sustainable building but didn't give us any parameters. So we just designed what we thought would work. In terms of sustainability, we went a long way. However, if there'd been a bit more pressure, I'm pretty sure we could have gone even further.

What are the key levers of change?

AG   I think that both bottom-up and top-down levers are important. As far as the energy debate goes, the real changes have come from top-down regulations. There have been lots of little changes, like recycling. People have always done a bit of recycling, but until you have a top-down regulation that says you have to and we're going to provide you with the facilities to do it, it doesn't really happen on a large scale. Similar mechanisms should be applied to the building sector. Life cycle assessments, for instance, should become mandatory so that we have to think more about where the materials come from and how we can use them in different ways.

Ultimately, with legislation as a driver, architects and design teams can work creatively within predetermined constraints. Architects love constraints! If one of the constraints is changing how we see photovoltaics, then architects will find a way of dealing with that. I have confidence in their ability to adapt and change and be creative with what they've got to work with, but they definitely need to be motivated by creative constraints.

If we want to change architects' mindset, then planning and regulations must change. The price of electricity doesn't change an architect's mindset, but it might change that of the client, who will ask for something different. If you take reference values for insulation performance, for instance, those regulations mean people have to design buildings in a different way and that they're aware of that parameter from day one. Glazing is another emblematic example. Regulations are becoming stricter in terms of glazing, but technology is advancing, which is allowing the sector to meet these strict requirements. So immediately there is a driver that's changing the glazing and manufacturing market. We've seen all sorts of innovations in glazing technology as a result of these dynamics. A good example of this technological progress is The Shard tower in London, where we also collaborated with architect Renzo Piano [Figure E]. The curtain-like walls we created (the size of glass panes, the selective coatings, the multiple glass layers with automatically-controlled roller blinds) wouldn't have even been imaginable when I joined Arup in 1979. These technological advances have made a huge difference not only in the energy performances of the facade, but also in its architectural expression—the "glass shard" look, as Renzo Piano likes to call it.

Photovoltaics are another good example in a 2050 perspective. They've become increasingly efficient in recent years. The specific technologies we're looking at today have probably reached a peak, but new technologies will soon emerge and replace the existing ones in terms of efficiency. The use of photovoltaics will undoubtedly greatly increase in the future [Figure F].

I'd like to insist here on the importance of addressing sustainability issues early on in the design process. About ten years ago, I led a project at Arup wherein we put together a framework of issues for each project that we wanted to address from the early design phase. We had six basic objectives: carbon, water, materials, community and the environment, climate change and operations. We've pretty much revamped that strategy, based on the UN's 17 Sustainability Goals. Our desire to take up some

"If we want to change architects' mindset, then planning and regulations must change."

E The Shard, London (United Kingdom)
   Renzo Piano Building Workshop arch., 2012

F Predicted annual worldwide BIPV commercial market revenue, 2018–2026
   The revenue is split between roofing, walling and glass

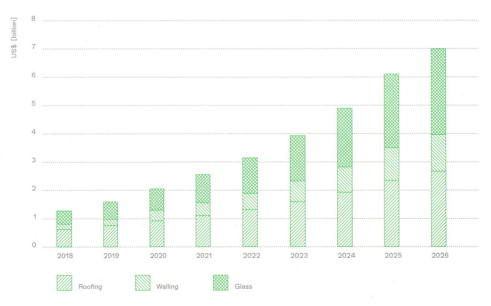

of these issues is certainly growing and, at the same time, legislation is pushing us toward that, which is a good thing.

I think it's also very important to have a bottom-up approach to raise awareness and get people thinking about sustainability. One of the main areas I see considerable change in throughout Europe is education. Children now learn about sustainability and energy from a very young age at school. As they grow up, they'll have a different view of these things. There will be more bottom-up pressure in the future.

Will professions change?
Will new professions emerge?

AG   I think they already have, meaning that the relative importance of different professions has changed. From my experience and what I know, great importance is being placed on mechanical engineering and building physics because they have led the push towards sustainability, along with the areas of energy and water. Many of my structural colleagues are now thinking about sustainability as they explore new materials and, as such, have come to be very much part of the conversation. As things change, the importance of various disciplines does shift. However, as I mentioned before, I think the two crucial elements for enacting change are an integrated team and a strong understanding of the sustainability drivers among the team members.

What I like to say is, "Let's imagine what we could do on this project!" because we can always work backwards from that point. Again, that's backcasting. Let's imagine what we could do and then see what's feasible or cost-effective. Everybody in the design team needs to be part of that discussion.

Another relevant aspect—and I don't know whether it's true or not in the rest of Europe, but I think it is true in the UK—is that there has been some real foot dragging in the architecture schools. There are many architecture courses in the UK that don't teach anything at all on sustainability, and the ones that do don't put much emphasis on it.

I think schools have been quite slow in that area, but I can tell from my teaching experience that things are changing. At the School of Architecture and the Built Environment at Nottingham University, where I teach as a Professor of Environmental Design, we really try to develop this integrated view of building design. This requires not only an architectural concept, but also a real understanding of the technologies involved in buildings to get a better outcome.

So, education is still an obstacle?
Are there others?

AG   Yes, there are fairly strict regulations about architecture education that need to change so as to encourage students to think more about sustainability. There's been a bit of a change in the willingness to consider the topic in architectural design

> "Students should definitely be scored on sustainability criteria for their final studio projects."

studios, but it should really be a clear part of the curriculum. Students should definitely be scored on sustainability criteria for their final studio projects.

Not long ago, I gave a talk at a conference with a number of UK architecture schools. I was very surprised to discover that most didn't have a sustainability programme. When young architects begin their careers, it takes them a long time to get to the point where they can express their ideas, even if their ideas are wonderful, because they're always working for somebody who's more senior and makes the decisions. I certainly see a real change in the view of sustainability among the architects I work with.

Sustainability principles must become an inherent part of our thinking, and we have to understand what they mean in terms of design. One of the problems is that, in the past, the majority of good examples of sustainability were architectural eyesores. I think we've turned that corner a bit and are getting some really good architecture now. Another big problem I've seen many times is that architects who've jumped on the sustainability bandwagon talk about the sustainability of their project, but their projects aren't really sustainable at all. You read about them in magazines, we give them awards, but the projects don't really do justice to sustainability. I think the whole industry has to change a bit and become more honest about what's really been achieved.

Do you think monitoring and post-occupancy evaluations could help overcome this obstacle?

AG   Maybe, but it's surprisingly difficult to use those types of approaches. We've done monitoring on only one or two projects, and to tell you the truth, I always worry that we don't do enough of it. The main reason is simply that you have to persuade your client to want to do it. If your client owns and operates the building, he or she might be inclined to do it. However, if someone else is managing the building, they're never keen to do it. Also, it's expensive because monitoring, analyzing, receiving users' reactions and measuring energy performances take time.

Maybe more embedded technology would be helpful here, by making measuring easier. For instance, we have prototype desks here at Arup where every single thing is monitored and can be controlled with your phone. So, we can see exactly how much energy our computer, light, etc. use. We did this project for ourselves but also did it for a big dotcom company. They've installed this kind of desk in some of their offices in London, so we're going to be able to get detailed feedback. The temperature and lighting can be somewhat controlled. Every action is recorded. For that particular project, that area of the building has battery storage. When electricity prices go up, they automatically switch to battery energy so that all the laptops run on batteries for a time. In addition, the whole building uses Direct Current (DC) power versus Alternating Current (AC). The advantage is that everything can be plugged into USB sockets, including the lighting.

Here again, this is a good illustration of a technology that gives us the ability—though the savings are not immediate—to monitor use so we can think about how to control, turn off and match loads based on what's available.

"Architecture is not the work of an architect; it is the product of a community."

Kengo Kuma

Kengo Kuma earned a degree in Architecture from the University of Tokyo in 1979, after which he moved to New York City to continue his studies at Columbia University as a visiting researcher. In 1987, he founded the "Spatial Design Studio" and in 1990 opened his own office, "Kengo Kuma & Associates," which employs over 200 architects in Tokyo, China, and Paris and designs projects of various type and scale throughout the world. He is also a professor at the Graduate School of Architecture at the University of Tokyo and oversees architectural, urbanity and design research projects within his own laboratory, Kuma Lab.

Interview date and location:
11 January 2018, Geneva, Lobby of the Hotel Cornavin

> How would you define sustainability within the built environment in a 2050 perspective?

KG For me, sustainability is mainly about material. During the 20th century, people started considering steel and concrete as the only building materials available. Unfortunately, those kinds of materials destroy architectural diversity. Industrial materials are cold, hard and not comfortable for human beings. Moreover, they hamper buildings' flexibility and have created a disconnect between architecture and location.

Prior to the 20th century, architecture was deeply connected to place and to the artisans living there and working in the building sector. Industrial materials have completely destroyed that kind of connection between place, buildings and people, which I believe is fundamental in terms of sustainability. For me, sustainability is neither about CO_2 nor about global warming, but rather the relationship to place.

Nowadays, and looking ahead to 2050, I feel people are more and more willing to focus on this relationship to place. Some clients are really looking for a close connection between the place and the project, not only in Japan but all over the world.

> In this context of "relationship to place," what are the major challenges and opportunities for the built environment?

KG Using local materials is a tough challenge because it often leads to increased costs. However, if we can reconnect to this relationship to place, craftsmen will once again find their place in the construction industry. At present, the number of craftsmen working in this industry is steadily declining. However, renewing this link with them will mean their return to construction sites. This shift, which will greatly impact the economic dimension, will also reduce building costs. I'm very optimistic for the future.

> If we look more closely at the building scale, what could be the role of buildings within cities and society in general?

KG Buildings' role should be dictated by construction processes. During the 20th century, the industrial era totally separated humans from production processes by limiting their role to the buying and selling of products made in factories. Buildings were also considered as nothing more than large commodities that could be bought or sold for more or less money. No one cared about the construction or maintenance processes. However, it is through these processes, which are becoming increasingly important, that people can create communities that allow architecture to truly exist. Architecture can thus become a node that enriches community ties. I have worked very closely with communities, often conducting workshops and trying to listen to craftsmen's opinions. From this experience, I came to the conclusion that architecture is not the work of an architect; it is the

"Sustainability is neither about CO_2 nor about global warming, but rather the relationship to place."

A China Academy of Art's Folk Art Museum, Hangzhou, Zhejiang (China)
Kengo Kuma & Associates, 2015

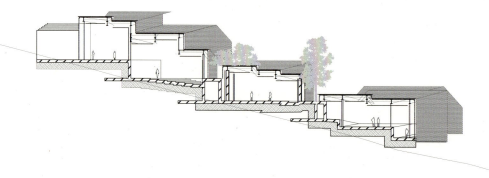

product of a community. In my opinion, the construction process itself is more important than the result.

This view of architecture as being more process-oriented than result-oriented actually comes from Buddhist philosophy. In Buddhism, especially Zen, the process of co-working is essential. Buddhist monks work together, cook together, clean together, etc. This is one of the most important aspects of their religion. So basically, one of our major challenges is rediscovering how to work together and create meaning—and architecture—together.

> Do you think the design process will evolve in that direction?

KG   Yes, absolutely. In my office, for example, we're very concerned with the design process. As I mentioned before, we often organize workshops to involve the community, artisans, manufacturers, etc. It's important to work together with these actors from the project's inception. If we include them in the process once the design has been completed, it's already too late. However, by working together with craftsmen and manufacturers from the very beginning, we can find a unique solution for each building. In our projects, each solution is unique. We don't want to repeat ourselves; we want to develop a specific solution for each project with the team. When we reach this unique solution, this strengthens ties within the entire team. This is when the building process gets really enjoyable!

A remarkable thing we've observed with many projects is the continuity of these close ties, even after completion of the building. These conditions allow for the emergence of a cohesive community with the building as its focal point.

Furthermore, we often return to our buildings in order to get feedback from the community and users. Though informal, this feedback is very valuable for our subsequent projects. To me, that kind of direct communication is more important than any feedback we could get via the Internet, for instance.

> As an architect who works all over the world, do you have easy access to local artisans and local resources? Isn't there a paradox between the local and global dimensions?

KG   Well, we try to work with local craftsmen, but that's not always possible. However, I wouldn't call it a paradox. On the contrary, working at the global scale can also be beneficial. For some projects, for instance, we ask artisans from elsewhere to collaborate in the building process. In a new art gallery we're currently building in Paris, for example, we involved a craftsman from Japan who's a rice paper expert. In this sense, this mechanism can stimulate local craftsmanship and foster exchanges within this community.

Our project for the Folk Art Museum on the China Academy of Arts campus in Hangzhou, China, is another good example of how architecture can enhance the local community and culture ^(Figure A). The main idea behind the museum was to focus on the small village community. We tried to value the site—a former tea field forming a hillside—to the best of our ability by respecting the landscape and intricate topography. The project is an aggregation of small units with individual roofs, which, from afar, looks like a village. The roofs are made with local Chinese ceramic roof tiles, which are actually quite beautiful—more so than the Japanese ones! In Japan, roof tiles are produced in big factories and are all the same colour, size and texture. In China, small villages still produce their own ceramic tiles by hand, which creates great diversity and richness in terms of textures. We also covered the outer vertical wall with a screen of tiles suspended by stainless wires, which controls the amount of sunlight that comes in. We wanted to work with old local tiles for both the roofs and the screen so that the architecture would naturally blend in with the landscape.

What role does technology play in your approach? How do you foresee this evolution?

KG	I don't want to separate technology from tradition in my work. A good example of this is the "Under One Roof" project on the Ecole polytechnique fédérale de Lausanne (EPFL) campus in Switzerland ^(Figure B). I like to describe this project as a combination of traditional materials and new technology. We started by asking ourselves what were the most important materials in Swiss villages. The answer was quite clear and compelling: wood and stone. These two materials are indeed essential to the architectural vocabulary in Switzerland. So we decided to use wood for the structure and exterior. We selected timbers commonly found in Switzerland to create a space with an air of local warmth, softness and humanity. For the roof we used stone, which echoes the traditional methods used in vernacular Swiss houses. The 235 meter-long pitched roof provides shelter for pedestrians and houses the Arts & Science Pavilion, the Technology & Information Gallery and the Montreux Jazz Cafe. The use of traditional local materials didn't stop us from using a unique engineering approach for the structure itself. The building's width constantly changes, so that the span of each of the fifty-seven structural portals is different. So we developed a new solution by combining wood and steel. By changing the proportions of the wood/steel composition, we were able to maintain the exact same section throughout the building. Hence, we designed a modular envelope that could be pre-fabricated.

Furthermore, I'm convinced that if we want to apply new technology in our buildings, then some kind of craftsmanship will always be needed to implement it. A good example is the "fa-bo" project, a fabric laboratory in Japan ^(Figure C) where we used carbon fibre on the exterior of the building to ensure its

B Under One Roof – project for the EPFL ArtLab, EPFL Campus, Lausanne (Switzerland)
Kengo Kuma & Associates, 2016

C   Komatsu Seiren Fabric Laboratory fa-bo, Ishikawa (Japan)
    Kengo Kuma & Associates, 2015

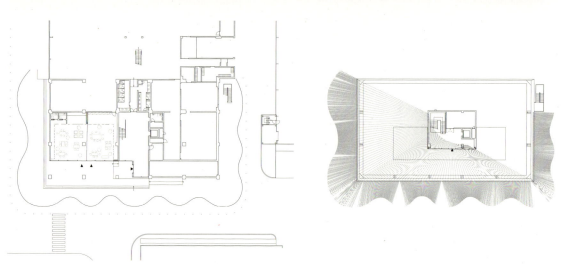

seismic reinforcement. Carbon fibre is very contemporary technology, but to produce the strands, we asked for the support of a craftsman. In this respect, both technology and architecture are always executed by a human hand. In my opinion, this isn't going to change in the future, as traditional, contemporary and future technologies can't be separated! New technologies will be invented, but if we want to use these technologies we'll always need a human hand. In this sense, vernacular and contemporary architecture cannot be separated. On the contrary, what we should be looking to do is to integrate these two dimensions.

What's your opinion of technology within buildings?

KG I'm not very interested in technology within the building itself, for instance, automated devices that turn lights on or off or control windows — in other words, controlling systems that do what users would normally do. I want to encourage users to use their own hands and to feel the space with their own body. We need to use our bodies and will need to do so even more in the future. Architecture should encourage this kind of direct contact between body and material.

> "Architecture should encourage this kind of direct contact between body and material."

In my firm we don't use technology to calculate the precise energy balance of new buildings. However, using local materials naturally supports the environmental dimension of sustainability. If we use local wood, for instance, we'll reduce not only the building's grey energy compared to industrial materials, but also the energy required for transporting the materials. We don't calculate the figures but rather use our intuition. Intuition has always been and will remain important for architecture and design.

> "Intuition has always been and will remain important for architecture and design."

Do you think users' expectations and behaviours will change in the future?

KG Yes, very much so. Designers, builders and users have been completely separated since the industrial era. In the future, they must be more connected, or even merge. In our projects, for instance, we try to involve users not only in the design process, but also in the building process. In this sense, buildings can become true nests for their occupants — just like animals! Animals design, build and use their own "homes." This kind of system is ideal for architectural design.

Hence, the role of architects is to provide users with a "good" example. Architects can demonstrate and act as team leaders but should never be separate from users, as is too often the case. That's why education in architecture has to change radically. In the 20th century, architects' education centered around design. Design, however, doesn't need to be taught. I try to teach my students how to communicate with the people and with materials. We do workshops with our students that integrate players from the building community so that they have the opportunity to learn to talk to users and communicate with people directly. We also teach our students the principles of

D GC Prostho Museum Research Center, Aichi (Japan)
Kengo Kuma & Associates, 2010

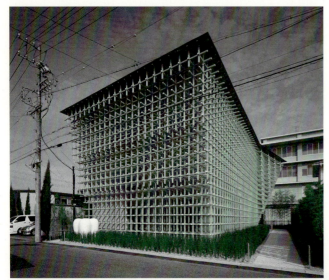
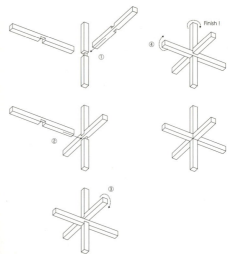

self-construction. Take the Cidori Pavilion at the Milano Exhibition, designed in 2007. Cidori is the name of a small Japanese toy for children. It's based on a traditional technique of lacing thin rectangular wooden sticks into a lattice by making a special notch in the wood. We adapted this into a three-dimensional system to create a strong, modular, easily dismantlable structure without any nails, screws or glue. In collaboration with Japanese carpenters, we asked our students to build a pavilion following the Cidori system so they could directly communicate with the material and use their hands. That kind of direct communication was completely neglected during the 20th century, which was all about one-sided communication from teachers to students. Today, we need to renew this link.

This successful experience with my students using the Cidori technique inspired several other projects in my firm, including furniture and buildings ^{Figure D}.

How about interdisciplinarity? Is it an important aspect of your teaching and work?

KG In Japanese education, engineers and architects study in the same universities, which is not the case in the American system, for instance, where there continues to be complete division between design and engineering. I believe that interdisciplinary education is very helpful for teaching architectural design in its entirety. Design should definitely be integrated with other disciplines. In my teaching, I often teach workshops together with engineers.

We apply the same principles in my firm: we work with integrated teams of architects, engineers and experts from other backgrounds. There's resistance, of course. From my experience at the University, I've observed that engineers are willing to co-teach with us designers, but that, unfortunately, architects are sometimes reluctant to do the same. Many obstacles also exist in practice, in large part because the building sector is very conservative. The internal organization of construction companies is based on the separation between designers and engineers, so neither is eager to exchange. Interdisciplinarity is truly a challenge: old habits die hard, and it's not easy to change the system! In the end, I'm confident that things will slowly change. It takes time.

"It's going to take some time for people to see that there's not much value in creating living environments that are only sculptural."

Ali Malkawi

Ali Malkawi is a professor of Architectural Technology at the Harvard Graduate School of Design and founding director of the Harvard Center for Green Buildings and Cities. His research specifically addresses computational simulation, building performance evaluation and energy conservation. Trained as an architectural engineer, he also works as a consultant on various building typologies across multiple scales.

Interview date and location:
20 April 2017, Cambridge (US), Harvard University

What's your definition of a sustainable built environment in a 2050 perspective?

AM I always think about the sustainability of the built environment in terms of its impact on its surroundings. If you're building a structure or city, how can you design it so that it will have a positive or, at the very least, a neutral impact on the environment?

Of course, resources are an important part of the equation. It's not only about the building or the city itself; it's about the resources used within that built environment to sustain it and that have an impact not only on their surroundings, but also at different scales, including time. Take materials, for example: you should consider how much impact they'll have both on the building's immediate surroundings and their place of origin, and how long it's going to take to balance their extraction.

What are the challenges to reaching this vision?

AM I think the science is there, but the technology required to implement certain scientific solutions is limited by political will, financial constraints and industry fragmentation and pressure. The other very fundamental issue is the relative lack of education, not among experts but among those applying sustainability concepts. We know what sustainability is, I think we think we understand it, but when we try to apply it, the expertise is not integrated in a way that benefits the project.

From an engineering perspective, this issue has a longer history due to how we think about buildings as enclosures that are completely dissociated from their environment. This is the result of how things have developed over the past 100 years or so, with heating and cooling, air conditioning and the technology that came along with it, regulations in the United States versus those in Europe, the influence of certain trends and how people have been educated. The engineering field has become increasingly responsible for ensuring that sustainability issues are being addressed. As such, architects have played a smaller role. More successful projects would be predominantly orchestrated by architects who are able to drive the project to the goal initially agreed upon.

As a consultant working on building projects and developing standards, I think what's hard is figuring out how to get back to the fundamentals and parsing through the noise. The field is oversaturated; suddenly everybody's a self-proclaimed sustainability expert. I think fundamental knowledge isn't really finding its way out.

What are the opportunities for facing these challenges?

AM There are some excellent examples of what can be done and what needs to be done in terms of efficiency. We must concentrate on the positive aspects to ensure that they're highlighted and replicated. For instance, if we look at the energy aspect of sustainability relative to the built environment, I think it's not so much about energy production alone as it is about how you utilize it in the most efficient manner. Engineers are inclined to go with what they

"It's not so much about energy production alone as it is about how you utilize it in the most efficient manner."

know in terms of production modes and efficient, sustainable, low-impact generation systems, and to optimize that. Trying to utilize the available resources in the most efficient way is much harder because the issues are design-related. There are many more variables. Because it's a more complicated issue, one tends to leave it aside and focus on the relatively easier engineering problem of producing clean, safe energy.

It's a question of supply and demand. Minimizing the demand as much as possible has many benefits — not only energy, but also social, health and well-being. If you have a poorly-built house, use air conditioning, etc., and you want to make it zero carbon, what you might do if you have a piece of land is put a bunch of photovoltaics on it and generate enough for that house. But this doesn't target efficiency, so is it the right approach? If you redesign the home to make it more harmonious with its environment, using natural ventilation, reducing the need for electrical lighting, etc., the efficiency achieved has multiple implications at different levels that cannot be considered by only focusing on supplying the demand of the existing condition.

> Would you say then that sometimes we're not aiming at the right targets or using the right metrics to quantify what good performance is?

AM   Yes, and what's good not just for the individual object you're trying to optimise, but at different levels — the neighbourhood, city, occupants and their health. A better design that's integrated in its environment not only reduces the need for resources, but also improves the quality of the built environment for its inhabitants, and that's very important. For example, if you use electrical lighting in the daytime (run on your own photovoltaic production) and don't have access to daylight, your psychological well-being will be different than if you had access to natural light, which uses less energy. This offers a different, added value whose quantification is essential because it trickles up to how regulations are developed.

> How do you address these issues in your work as a researcher and professor here?

AM   I can give a few examples of the many research projects we conduct here. From a computational perspective, we're looking at how to quantify uncertainties in building performances to help run them more efficiently. We lack computational environments that support rapid decision making for building design or performance assessment. At the Harvard Center for Green Buildings and Cities (CGBC), we focus on data-driven (versus simulation-based) models for buildings and cities, and are pursuing research to develop modeling methods that can take uncertainties, including human behaviour and local conditions, into account. The goal is to substantially reduce these uncertainties and to have better predictability models. So, we're collaborating with different researchers including mathematicians and computer scientists from the Harvard community and beyond.

Another project I have designed that we're working on is how we can apply our ideas and existing technology for building retrofitting. Working as a large team and in collaboration with leading firms from various regions including Scandinavia and the US, we have retrofitted a typical pre-1940s house in Cambridge (MA) into a functional office for up to 40 researchers and staff. The building will serve as the headquarters for the Harvard CGBC, the institute I founded. This first-of-its-kind instrument and laboratory is called the HouseZero project [Figure A]. By coupling contemporary technologies with better design, the goal is to create a fully passive building that uses almost no heating or cooling, with 100% daylight autonomy and 100% natural ventilation and zero emission, including the embodied energy in materials. It's much more challenging to do so in existing buildings, but we want to prove that it's possible. By doing so, we can address the problem of inefficient buildings, which account for vast amounts of energy use and carbon pollution worldwide.

The building is "over sensed," so we'll be generating a lot of data that will enable it to adjust itself, inform the creation of data-driven software and CGBC research on actual data and simulated environments. While the building itself functions as a testbed, HouseZero also features a flexible, highly-controlled and monitored experimental lab that is hardwired to the building's energy exchange system. The lab space is connected to an ultra-efficient structure that allows for experimentation, testing and optimisation of new, intelligent technologies, facades and materials. These will serve to inspire the next generation of ultra-efficient buildings by utilising data, artificial intelligence and a new generation of materials.

Of course, this is a demonstration and laboratory project. However, since some of our interventions are fairly standard (for instance, adding insulation), we believe that certain strategies could be applied in the retrofitting of buildings in the United States. This would lead to significant energy savings, lower operating costs, and a better environment for occupants.

From your experience, what are the key drivers of change?
AM   In addition to the bottom-up approach, the top-down approach is definitely important because the industry is very fragmented. What would be wonderful—and things seems to be moving in this direction—is if research and development could influence policy.

In academia, students generally look to magazines, journals and star-architects. There are few examples wherein environmental issues have been the focus of the agenda and performance becomes part of the design. There are still people who revere those designs, which have very little to do with the environment. I think that's changing, but it's going to take some time for people to see that there's not much value in creating living environments that are only sculptural. The artistic dimension and environmental considerations should no longer be seen as mutually exclusive; it's possible to embrace both.

A

HouseZero, Cambridge (USA)
Harvard Center for Green Buildings and Cities (CGBC) and Snøhetta arch., 2018

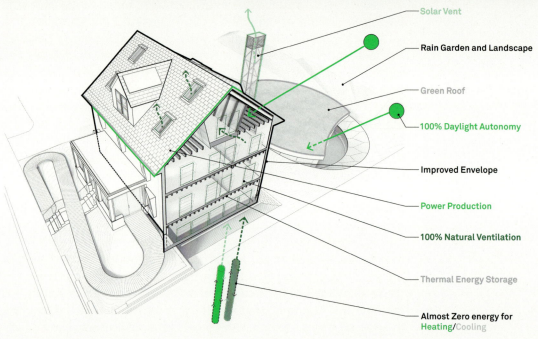

- Solar Vent
- Rain Garden and Landscape
- Green Roof
- 100% Daylight Autonomy
- Improved Envelope
- Power Production
- 100% Natural Ventilation
- Thermal Energy Storage
- Almost Zero energy for Heating/Cooling

There are not a lot of precedents in terms of good examples, but I think we're starting to see more and more as people progress along the learning curve. However, there's no good information available about the actual performances of these structures and how their environment reacts. They're mainly expressed through images. We lack monitoring, post-occupation and real feedback that would allow people to utilize this information to improve things. The feedback loop is very slow.

Will the architectural expression of buildings change?

AM   It doesn't have to change. I think we're going to start seeing — and in fact have already started seeing — buildings that, from an architectural expression perspective, are still very influential and engaging, and at the same time high-performing. You won't have to see their performance to know it's there. And that's what's lacking in the overwhelming majority of buildings. There's only a handful of examples out of millions of buildings— it's incredibly disproportionate. Only a few out of the millions might be considered "good." Globalization hasn't helped that much: the sway of companies that say "air-based systems filtration is the way to go, close it and it will be much better" is still strong.

How about the design process? Will it change?

AM   I think we are heading back to what we used to do before the computational revolution, back to sketches, models and fundamentals. Computation is good because you can probably accelerate certain processes, but we know and understand its limitations. This includes computational simulation, where most of my work lies. Parametric design analysis is still very simple and not holistic in terms of how we build buildings; you cannot generate high performance building designs based on parametric models. We are going back to using these tools and techniques in their most efficient way, but also going back to fundamentals. There is a recalibration going on, but it is very slow compared to other industries.

Regarding the use of technology and computational tools, most performance tools aren't designed for architects. There are two areas of application. For existing structures, I think analysis-based computational tools are advancing steadily to solve engineering problems. We're using sensors connected to computational tools as well as artificial intelligence — which is back, though we thought it was dying as its funding radically declined twenty years ago — in academia and research. The second area is the design of new structures, where computation is still lagging. There's an evolution in data sharing systems such as Building Information Modeling (BIM) that help in the production aspect of coordinating large, complex projects. In terms of helping with the design, it's still very elementary. Nobody is really pushing for that. It's mostly academics. And progress is very slow.

"We are heading back to sketches, models and fundamentals."

"I've always believed that a simple building is beautiful."

Edward Ng

Edward Ng is Yao Ling Sun Professor of Architecture at the Chinese University of Hong Kong, where he leads research on topics including solar access and daylighting, urban climatic mapping and climate change. Trained as an architect with a doctoral degree from the University of Cambridge, he conducts humanitarian work with his students while also working as a practicing architect and an environmental consultant to various Asian governmental bodies.

Interview date and location:
4 July 2017, Edinburgh,
Passive Low Energy Architecture Conference

> What's your definition of a sustainable built environment in a 2050 perspective?

EN   My definition is very similar to everybody's definition: to live within our limits and resources, and not to spend my son's inheritance. Scientifically speaking, we know very clearly what we have. Now, we must find a way to live within that.

> What are the main challenges and opportunities with regard to a sustainable built environment?

EN   There are many, but one of the biggest challenges, in my view, is that people in general are not aware of the urgency of the problem. We've been living a certain way of life—based mostly on economic development—for the past hundred years. So, our value system is still very much like it was during the industrial age. Everyday we look at how the stock market goes up or down; we never look at how CO_2 goes up or down^{Figure A}.

It's changing the mindset of society that is the major challenge. It is extremely difficult for people to change their mindset. That's why the government doesn't want to change: because people don't want to change, or don't know how to. They're not looking for that.

Some countries have greater awareness of energy and environmental issues, like Germany for instance, or northern European countries like Denmark, Sweden and Norway. In countries like this, where people are very aware and appreciate the urgency of the matter, policies are moving faster. Whereas in some countries like the United States, it's not that they don't know how to change, but rather don't want to^{Figure B}. The value system is such that they want to go on living life as usual. In Asia, it's more problematic because we want to live like Americans, so we're expanding.

> What role can buildings play? Can they educate people?

EN   A building can educate people, but people will always backslide. If you design a building and try to educate people about how to change their habits, they'll either complain or cut corners. Relying on buildings alone is not sufficient, as the backslide effect is very common.

I have a good example to illustrate this mechanism. I teach in a five-storey building. I asked the building manager to shut down the lift so that students would have to walk upstairs. Five storeys is nothing! But the students complained they had to walk from the ground floor to the first floor! They didn't want to. They complained so much that the president of the University said that we couldn't stop people from using the lift. The most common answer I got from students is, "I've paid my school fees. That included lifts."

People won't change their habits unless their way of life is jeopardized. Otherwise, it's somebody else's problem. As I said,

> "Everyday we look at how the stock market goes up or down; we never look at how CO_2 goes up or down."

A Dow Jones Industrial Average (Index) vs Atmospheric CO_2 concentrations (ppm), 2016–2017

— Atmospheric CO_2 concentrations [ppm] derived from in situ air measurements at Mauna Loa Observatory, Hawaii (USA)
— Dow Jones Industrial Average (DJIA)

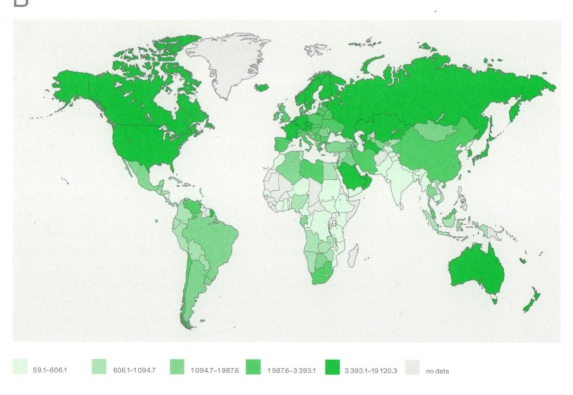

B Global energy consumption per capita (kg of oil equivalent per capita), 2010

59.1–606.1 | 606.1–1 094.7 | 1 094.7–1 987.6 | 1 987.6–3 393.1 | 3 393.1–19 120.3 | no data

Thinking

> "The space must be designed such that people will enjoy the walk."

the problem lies in mindsets and lifestyles, not technology. Once you understand that you can easily walk up five storeys instead of taking the lift, then staircases can be better designed. The space must be designed such that people will enjoy the walk. But even if you do that, people will still complain that they don't have a lift, no matter how wonderful the staircase is. They still want the lift because of their lifestyle.

What are the major obstacles to the construction and evolution of buildings?

EN   I believe that in terms of construction, design, etc., technology can get it almost right. Regarding management and control systems, however, their responsiveness and user-friendliness still need some fine-tuning. But the building envelope and systems are more or less there.

The difficulties I find and that a lot of research indicates is that, when a system or building is dependent on how people use it, then the two things don't necessarily match up. Therefore, energy wastage is not a by-product of the system itself, but rather of people's improper use of it. My students are perfectly capable of turning on the air conditioning (AC) and opening the windows at the same time because they think they need better "fresh" air. Because the AC provides coolness, they don't mind the hot air coming in from outside. If it gets too hot, they simply turn up the AC because they think having this combination of "fresh" air and AC is best.

So, the obstacle is people's misuse of buildings or lack of understanding of how it works. For example, when you buy a car, you get a manual that tells you which switch does what. If you buy a new computer with a new operating system, you get training. How often do you buy a house and get training on how to live in it? Never. There isn't even a manual that teaches you how to use your building properly. For example, if a building is airtight and people don't realize that, then they can just open a window and all that airtightness is lost. What's the point of designing the best, most efficient, most sophisticated building if people don't know how to use it? People need to learn to use a good building properly. Otherwise, it's easy to turn it into a bad building.

What is technology's role?
Can it be used to make people more aware?

> "We have more technology than we need to solve the problem."

EN   Technology is there and isn't a problem. In fact, we have more technology than we need to solve the problem. Now, the question is how to solve the problem? Unless, of course, I'm wrong and there's some kind of what we call a "transformational technology" that itself solves the problem. For example, something that generates a lot of energy but no carbon dioxide. Maybe it will happen, who knows, but we shouldn't count on it.

In terms of technology for informing people, most information only reinforces what people already believe. People select the information they want instead of saying "Oh, I was wrong." This is how we collect and process information. We don't process information to prove ourselves wrong. That's the problem. More information may not be better; it may simply mean people are becoming more stubborn by reinforcing their own ideas. Therefore, you have to have some kind of disruptive education that tells you you're wrong, but we don't like that kind of education. If your mom tells you you're wrong, you won't talk to her for two weeks! It's human nature. We can't fight against human nature.

> How do you deal with all these challenges in your work?

EN   The way we do things is by designing simple buildings. We're very down to earth, and my projects are always very low-tech. We understand how people live, how they move in and out of the house, how they spend the day, how they read their newspaper, etc. The first step is understanding people, and then designing spaces using passive means: putting a window in the right place or creating a courtyard with appropriate proportions. We don't use smart systems for most of the work. Instead, we rely on building physics, meaning the building's envelope and geometry. We always observe people and how they behave, and then design something very simple that people can understand. Everyone can understand a window, but not everyone understands all these high-tech gadgets and buttons, which are very difficult to set, especially for older people.

We rely on passive design to solve most of our problems, but that mostly applies to the residential buildings I design, and not office buildings. Personally, I prefer residential buildings because they're closer to people. I feel like I can work better with a closer connection to the occupants.

> Your anti-seismic house in Guangming seems emblematic of these principles. Can you tell us more about that project?

EN   Yes, of course! The project [Figure C] started in 2014 after the devastating earthquake in Ludian County, China. When we ventured into Guangming village, we discovered that most of the rammed-earth houses had been destroyed. In collaboration with members of the local University of Kunming, who helped us connect with both villagers and the local government, we started investigating the shortcomings of these houses that had been destroyed. We also included experts in seismic-resistant design from the University of Cambridge in the team.

First and foremost, the house design had to be simple because we wanted the villagers to be able to build it themselves. Using our experts' input, we improved the earth mixture that existed onsite by increasing the resistance and workability of the material. Simplicity is also an important parameter for seismic-resistant design: simple geometries are more resistant than

"My projects are always very low-tech."

C Post-Earthquake Reconstruction Project in Guangming Village, Zhaotong (China)
The Chinese University of Hong Kong & Kunming University of Science and Technology arch., 2016

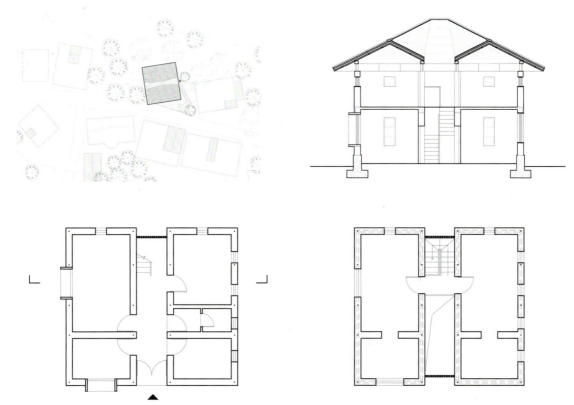

Edward Ng

complex ones. A square form, for instance, is always stronger. Even if the walls collapse, the pyramid-shaped roof will stay intact, allowing inhabitants to escape from the building uninjured. This is how we started our design—with a square block. Openings also required special attention: every time we create an opening in an earth wall, we weaken it. We had to surround the larger window openings with a concrete frame that would keep the window intact in case the walls started shaking.

But the challenge here wasn't just building a house that's resistant; above all, we wanted to build a house that its inhabitants would enjoy, in this case an elderly couple. We asked them what they needed for their daily lives and then designed the accommodations accordingly. We divided the square form into two blocks separated by an atrium space that is brightly lit by overhead lighting, and cool in summer and warm in winter thanks to the high thermal mass of the earth.

However, the project was more than just a single house; it's a prototype that can allow us to solve many problems in other parts of the world where earthquakes are an issue.

And how do you deal with commercial buildings?

EN	For commercial buildings, it's more difficult because the demands are greater and different. A house is for several people, who you can get to know. An office is for everybody, and you don't know everybody. It's more difficult to fine-tune your design for people in an office or school. For those, you may need to design different spaces—some hotter, some cooler—so that people can choose where they want to sit. The downside is that you waste a lot of space. I've done one or two institutional buildings. My approach has always been to create a range of spaces so that the occupants can move around. Instead of trying to create one space that will serve multiple functions, I create different spaces for different purposes. For institutional buildings, because they are so many more people in them and their uses are more unpredictable, the likelihood of using active systems is higher.

Do you use any tools, including digital tools?

EN	Yes, we have to use some simulation tools to help visualize performance. However, we know roughly how our designs perform, and are mainly looking for confirmation. We rarely change our designs because they're so simple that it's rare that anything goes wrong. A complicated design can often go wrong. For example, air can go in somewhere that you didn't expect it to. That means it's much more important to make a few iterations to make it right, and that takes time. If you're running out of time and have one month to create a design, and this is a five-month process, then you need to stop somewhere along the way that isn't optimal. Whereas if you design something simple, you know it works and only need to confirm that. You don't need to change it.

We also use digital tools to do post-occupancy monitoring. This is how we learn from our buildings. Most architects tend to design a building, take a picture and go away. They just don't care! In my office, we put sensors in our buildings and monitor them for at least a year. That way we know what works and what doesn't, and for the next building, we know how to adjust. That's what we do each time.

However, we don't rely purely on technology. We also go back to ask people what's good and what isn't. We learn from the people who use the building. I think this is a very important step for developing sustainable buildings. Feedback, which is neither complicated nor expensive, should be included in the design process. Sometimes the occupants tell you that you made a mistake, which is ok. The sensors are there to confirm our observations. It's rare that we have surprises because our buildings are so simple.

> As an architect, consultant and professor, what do you feel are the main drivers of change? Where can you have the most influence?

EN   In all three. As an architect, as we discussed earlier, you can understand how people live and how to live more sustainably through design.

As a consultant, you help different groups start the process; you teach practitioners the steps to take by pushing ideas that are easy to implement. Once they've started, at least they know what the next step is. For example, sometimes the government doesn't know how to proceed: it starts with the most difficult policy (which nobody follows anyway) and then gets stuck. We help the government draft simple policies so that people know how to begin and move on from there to more difficult policies.

In academia, when you educate, you transfer knowledge to younger generations. Education is the main thing we should get right. Unfortunately it's a long, slow process. By the time we educate, the battle is lost. I have no idea how we can fast-track education. Changing values and mindsets is a long-term process that takes several generations. Sometimes, it takes a disaster to change mindsets quickly, and we don't want a disaster.

> What can be done as part of architecture education?

EN   Instead of talking about form, geometry, composition or aesthetics, as most architecture schools do today, we need to come back to the basics. I've always believed that culture, history and theory are built on a foundation of natural laws. Natural laws are those that gave us the laws of physics, the environment and materials. If you understand those, you can see how all culture, history and proportions derive from that basis. For example, in a hot and dry climate, you always build your courtyard with vertical proportions. People now consider that as cultural because in other parts of the world, courtyards are always horizontal. So there are cultural differences, but culture is simply a response to the fundamental laws of how the sun moves. It's as simple as that.

My suggestion to architecture schools is to go back to the laws of nature and rediscover manmade laws based on those fundamentals. Discover how culture responds to the environment, how human lifestyles respond to culture, and how our aesthetic values are based on living and culture, and thus natural laws. Nowadays, many architects talk about aesthetics as though they were abstract. But they've got it backwards! That's how I see architectural education, but I'm quite sure some—or even many—architects wouldn't agree with me.

I've always believed that a simple building is beautiful. I like to call complicated buildings "Mickey Mouse" buildings. It's actually more difficult to make something simple. A building that responds to nature is architecture— and that is truly sustainable! Unfortunately, a lot of people like Mickey Mouse buildings because they're costly, exciting and nice to take pictures in front of, but they don't need to last. So, you can build another one in two years time to replace it. Maybe that's how we treat architecture—as a fashion. It's not about a place to live, it's a fashion statement. In the fashion world, you buy a new dress, take some pictures in it, throw it away and buy a new one. Even if the dress itself is sustainable, the process of renewing fashion isn't. That's my main comment on the architectural profession. Our mindset is not sustainable. I want my building to last 2 000 years, without maintenance. If you want that to happen, you only need a very simple construction detail. If you miss that detail, your building will last three months. Many architects don't pay attention to the small things. They want to design creative forms but don't look at the lines, so their buildings don't last. Their buildings leak, and they think, "Oh, that's normal. All buildings leak." But that's not true. All good residential buildings should not leak.

In this sense, many architects would benefit from rediscovering the benefits of vernacular architecture. However, with the waves of "icon" or "star" architecture, many architects refuse to follow tradition. They think they're creating something new, something unprecedented. The more sophisticated or stranger-looking the building, the more wonderful, interesting and iconic. However, actually building these designs and making them work is very difficult! Even after hiring the best engineers, they sometimes still don't work, so they have to rely on active systems. I think architects forgetting their past is a big problem.

"Sustainability is ok. Not being sustainable is bad. But then what's good?"

Susan Parnell

Susan Parnell is a professor of environmental and geographical sciences at the University of Cape Town in South Africa and member of the African Centre for Cities. Her research on contemporary urban policy extends beyond the academic environment through her involvement in non-governmental organizations (NGOs), governments and advisory panels at the national and international levels. She is particularly concerned with issues of poverty alleviation, environmental justice, gender equality and sustainability.

Interview date and location:
6 September 2016, Shanghai, Urban Transitions Global Summit

What is your definition of a sustainable built environment in a 2050 perspective?

SP   The Brundtland definition, which is based on resource constraint, is a useful definition of sustainability. However, we must go beyond that concept. There's merit in setting up systems that reproduce themselves, which is different than resource constraint. Sustainability should be about having enough adaptability to be reinvented. In terms of a building or neighbourhood, which can change fundamentally over time, this means that their use and/or identity can be reconfigured but that certain fundamental elements remain. I'm reluctant to use the word "resilience." Sustainability is multi-layered. We need to be sustainable 24/7, and over generations both environmentally and in terms of the institutions fueling this field. You really want something to be a bit more than sustainable. Sustainability is ok. Not being sustainable is bad. But then what's good? Perhaps we need some kind of "sustainability+ concept," whereby buildings can act as multipliers that give more than they take, be it in terms of energy, water, etc. What future generations value is the contribution from the past, a sense of intergenerational connectivity. So, making something sustainable could be translated into making something worth keeping.

What are the current and future issues? Is there a priority order in which to address them?

SP   There are many different kinds of issues! Common worldwide issues include poverty, inequality, violence, migration, refugees, racism and war. Then there are issues that are more specific to the Global North, such as neoliberalism, austerity, the ageing population [Figure A], de-industrialisation and exclusion, and those more specific to the Global South, like rapid urban growth [Figure B], unemployment [Figure C], youth bulge, tradition versus modernity, and so on. Moreover, future generations will have to deal with additional issues such as the loss of biodiversity [Figure D], disease, environmental risk and disaster, pollution and resource depletion. In view of these challenges, it is clear that cities require special attention.

In terms of hierarchy or which challenges must be addressed first, I think we have to mediate. It's important to be clear that—though we're always reluctant to say it—there are priorities. I don't think you can morally justify all of the effort, energy and funding being put into high-tech design and innovation if you don't, by the same token, provide for basic needs at the global level. All you're doing is increasing inequality. Your understanding becomes distorted if you don't keep coming back to some kind of social register, whether it's a register of inequality or intergenerational issues. You can work to make the life of the Copenhagen elite more carbon-neutral, but at what cost if you are not looking after the impoverished? It's not that you shouldn't innovate, but you should always have the bigger picture in mind.

"You can work to make the life of the Copenhagen elite more carbon-neutral, but at what cost if you are not looking after the impoverished?"

> "Buildings should delight, but they should also protect and inspire."

What will buildings' role be?

SP For me, what's really wonderful about the built environment is that it has the capacity to delight. When you go into a beautiful building, it's extraordinary. So buildings should delight, but they should also protect and inspire. They should be safe and accessible, provide natural air and light, and create opportunities for jobs in their construction and their use. In this sense, they should be productive, but not only energy-wise. I think the sustainability discourse has been encapsulated in the energy-water nexus, which is great, but there's much more to productivity than just those aspects. I'm more interested in asking, "What does that building or space do for the local economy?" For example, churches historically were quite productive. They were public spaces that conferred livelihood. We keep them because they are beautiful, but we need to rethink how they're used.

Another example of productive spaces is small squares where markets may periodically be held, where there's an infrastructure that can be used one way at night and another way by children during the day. Spaces that actually enable work.

Buildings must have a human element. They should make people feel dignified. For instance, we get very snobby about things like shopping malls, which most people tend to think are poorly designed and exclusionary. But I know people who go to shopping malls because they are public spaces that offer free music and clean toilets. The notion of the use value of a building—or a space—is another dimension that will remain essential in the future. When a building is empty much of the time, it means the society is producing more than it needs. When you go into an informal settlement, you never find an empty building. If you don't need something, what's its value? We have to be careful, though: "24/7 occupancy" is not necessarily the same as "value." You can use something only for special occasions, but you have to have that thing for special occasions.

What challenges do you see on the road to a "sustainable" (or "sustainable+") built environment?

SP Sometimes, ignorance. People simply don't know what needs to be done, or don't know what they are doing. Hence, knowledge of and attention to design are of the utmost importance. There is often a gap between conception and use. We have the idea that something will be used for X and it actually never is. That doesn't mean there's something inherently wrong with whatever it is (the product, etc.). However, some well-intentioned projects are completely unsustainable, for instance a new sports facility when there are already two in the neighbourhood. They can also be unsustainable if people haven't been taught how to use them.

There is also a lack of intelligent design and flexibility. We can't predict or know everything, but we should anticipate the

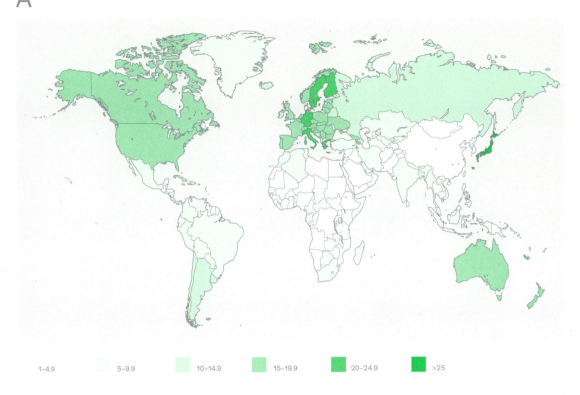

A Proportion of population aged 65 and over, 2017

1–4.9 | 5–9.9 | 10–14.9 | 15–19.9 | 20–24.9 | >25

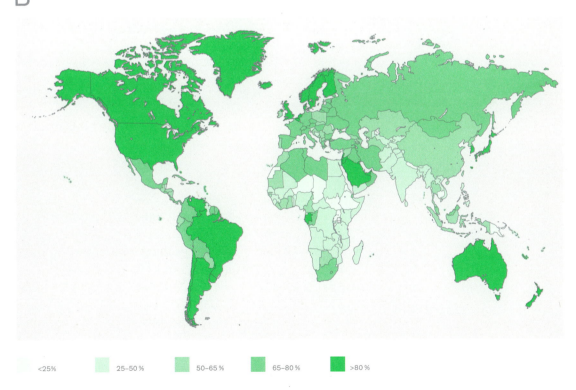

B Proportion of urban population, 2016

<25% | 25–50% | 50–65% | 65–80% | >80%

C Proportion of total unemployment (% of labor forces aged 15 and older), 2014

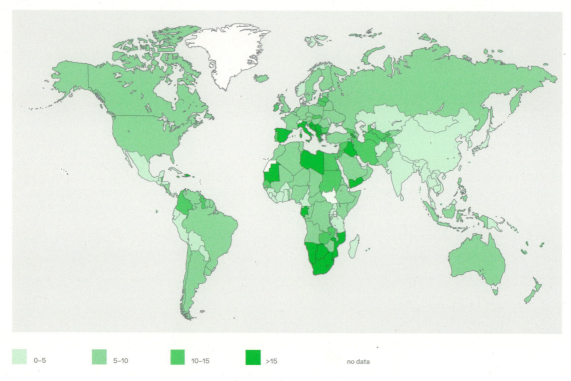

0–5   5–10   10–15   >15   no data

D Trend in population abundance for 14 152 populations of 3 706 species monitored across the globe between 1970 and 2012.

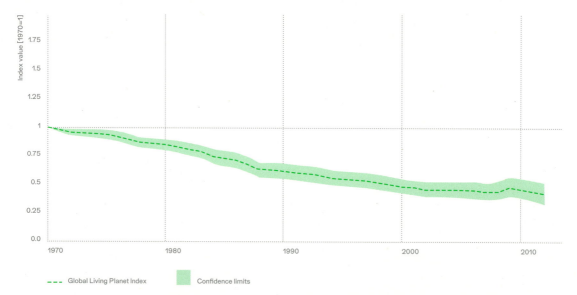

--- Global Living Planet Index   Confidence limits

134   Thinking

kind of flexibility we may need in the future. Things are often not sustainable enough; when they have to be re-invented, the cost-benefit of doing so doesn't make it worthwhile, so everything is lost. Especially in poor countries. Buildings are built in an improvised way and with a limited budget. It doesn't matter if they are temporary buildings. What does matter—a great deal even—is if they are expensive but of poor quality. If you can't afford concrete, don't use bad concrete. A budget shouldn't be pushed to the point where everything else (i.e. quality) is compromised.

In sustainability studies, people talk a lot about materiality and technology. For me, in a certain way, that's the least of it. Much more important is who goes in and comes out of the building, where they go and what they do for a living. It's about the type of community. That's what defines the kind of flexibility we need in our built environment.

Who are the key initiators of change?

SP I think it depends on where you're coming from. In some places, the professions are extremely well developed and what you might need is a profession to navigate the professions, because they're so powerful and their dominance isn't always geared towards the public good. I'd call for a recalibration of the relative power of different professions in a way that serves the public good. Perhaps we also need to develop a profession that orients the moral economy and sets the moral agenda and code. We lack direction in the philosophical sense. Given the situation, knowing what we know, if we continue making buildings and cities the way we do today, we're all going to die and bring down every other species with us. And yet, we hand this responsibility over to somebody who's trained to design buildings? They might be very good at making a building stand up but they're not philosophically or morally trained to help mediate crucial decisions. We need moral and technical leadership to inform us on what matters and what doesn't, and to guide us in terms of focus priorities.

What are the other drivers that could help us move ahead?

SP For one, a fiscal framework that defines what gets taxed and what doesn't, and how much things cost. Another is building codes and zoning, which I feel are fundamental. At the moment, building codes adhere to minimum standards, which are inappropriate because they are too high. We need to determine by how much can we lower these minimum standards. Then we need to introduce low maximum standards, for example for water consumption.

Finally, professional certification. In other words, what is included in a degree programme and what isn't. We need to adapt curriculums so as to teach responsibility. Do architects study philosophy and ethics? I think practices could very easily be shifted by changing the curriculum for civil engineers, architects, etc.

> "I'd call for a recalibration of the relative power of different professions in a way that serves the public good."

"The question isn't about low-tech or high-tech. The real question is knowing what to use according to the context."

Antoine Picon

Antoine Picon has been a professor of the History of Architecture and Technology at Harvard University's Graduate School of Design since 2002. With degrees in engineering, architecture and history, his current research interests include smart cities and digital culture in architecture, which are also the subjects of his latest books.

Interview date and location:
19 April 2017, Cambridge (US), Harvard University

What are the major challenges for the built environment in a 2050 perspective?

AP Figure A   There are several challenges. The first is obviously carbon and its role in global warming. This seems to be the biggest problem, particularly given that we're off to a bad start. We're pretty much backpedaling on all the limits we've set.

The second challenge that, systemically, is related to the first one is water and air quality. The third factor is materials. I think we're far from using materials in an optimal, thrifty way. The waste we produce is absolutely outrageous. We're pouring over half a tonne of concrete per inhabitant per year. That's a whole lot of concrete Figure B . So we'll probably have to radically change the materials we use.

Finally, let's not forget that the built environment is inhabited. So there aren't only technological challenges but also a need to change the way we live, our collective values, etc. Often, we mistakenly imagine that we only have to worry about technology when in fact we should think of it as inseparable from social aspects. Especially regarding issues in the built environment. We have a tendency to think like engineers. In reality, if you build a naturally-ventilated building but its occupants behave inappropriately, you haven't solved anything. Reforming our habits and values is fundamental.

> "Reforming our habits and values is fundamental."

How does the concept of smart cities, about which you have written extensively, relate to that of sustainable cities or buildings?

AP   I think these two concepts have largely converged. Today, most zero energy-type buildings are designed as though they were separate from the city, without solidarity with their surroundings, like some kind of Noah's Ark. We have to re-think this notion of solidarity between buildings. Until now, this solidarity has mainly been geometric (regarding urban compositions) and depended on a connection to the grid. In the future, we'll probably have to invent new ways of synergizing to build cities. One of the goals of smart cities is precisely to achieve sustainability objectives through more efficient and simultaneous management of the relationship between the environment, materials, processes, etc. The smart city problem also gives rise to environmental issues.

What complicates things, however, is the fact that digital technology consumes a lot of energy and requires the use of mixtures (welded pieces) that are very difficult to recycle. Thus, there is a conflict between the polluting, energy-intensive nature of these technologies and the fact that, if used wisely, they can improve efficiency and help in meeting environmental objectives. What I often say is that we're still in the gadget phase, where there's never enough technology. However, we'll soon have to exit the gadget phase and enter the actual smart city "savings mode,"

A Global CO$_2$ emissions (kt), 2011

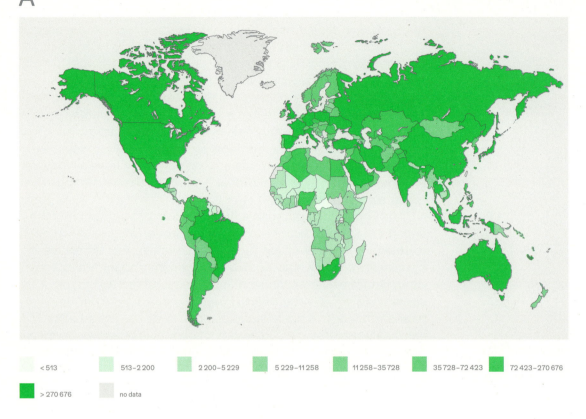

< 513 | 513–2 200 | 2 200–5 229 | 5 229–11 258 | 11 258–35 728 | 35 728–72 423 | 72 423–270 676

> 270 676 | no data

B Global cement production and associated CO$_2$ emissions, 1950–2016

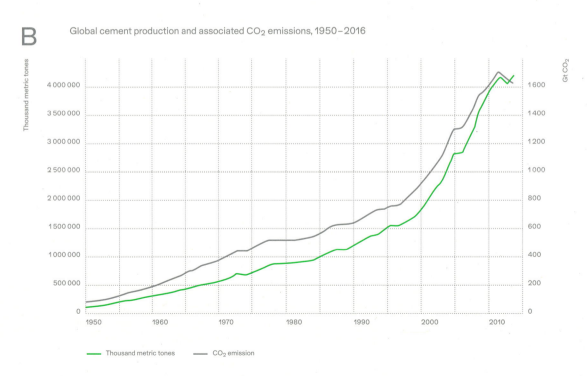

Thousand metric tones — CO$_2$ emission

where it's not necessarily good to put sensors everywhere. We'll have to determine what's good and bad usage of technology. Given that doing a Google search is equivalent to turning on an incandescent light bulb for just over fifteen seconds, not all Google searches are "good." Here as well, change must be driven by individuals' self-discipline.

> Do you think people realize the consequences of their acts, or is there a need for more education?

AP   People are not fully unaware, but as French philosopher and anthropologist Bruno Latour recently highlighted in one of his articles, there's no reason for people to be interested in climate change when they can clearly see that the world's most powerful people don't care about it.

I think there are multiple concurrent problems. It's obvious that there are issues in terms of education, but there's also the problem of the lack of political will and the need to reform the financial system. It's a paradox: we're in need of a planned economy more than ever. Yet, at the same time, planned economy has systematically failed. We're incapable of truly planning, yet we have to plan. We're incapable of putting into practice a real environmental policy that addresses inequality and other issues at the global scale—for now, at least. We can always remain optimistic and say that maybe one day there will be an event serious enough to get those in power to do something, but we're not there yet. It's not certain that we'll succeed in solving these problems, or that humanity still has millennia to come.

Our only hope is changing our imaginary and our values. Developed societies are going through a widespread, profound life crisis to which rampant consumerism doesn't fully respond. It's clear that the environmental concerns and expectations of younger generations are often linked to the desire for a change of lifestyles and values. I'd say perhaps our only hope is to give new meaning to our lives, both daily and in the long term.

> What role can buildings play?

AP   As we well know, the construction industry is a sector that is far from being neutral energy-wise. But beyond that, buildings are deeply linked to lifestyles. To come back to the subject of imaginaries and values without assuming a deterministic relationship between architecture, the city and lifestyles, there are still links to be made between the built fabric in which we live and the way we live. Hence the importance today of people who do exhibitions or build exemplary buildings that raise people's awareness. Given that buildings are intrinsically linked to the way we live, they have the power to play a significant educational role.

Besides, something we haven't been able to reverse is the fact that, let's face it, consuming in our consumer society is fun, even if it is the source of many of our existential crises. What environmentalists propose instead is less appealing. I think

"There's no reason for people to be interested in climate change when they can clearly see that the world's most powerful people don't care about it."

> "Architecture and the city should offer people a dimension of majesty and luxury."

architecture can respectfully contribute to the question of luxury. The question "what will remain of luxury in a world that has become frugal?" is a real obstacle to acceptability. When we hear "things will be the same as they are today, except that you won't have this or that," we're in no hurry to get there. In my opinion, architecture and the city should offer people a dimension of majesty and luxury.

It's not only about making beautiful buildings so people will love them and be willing to keep them for a long time. In my opinion, architecture can help to create a meaningful framework for human action, which is the number one condition for making life liveable. Through various dynamics, architecture has the potential to make life meaningful, which is a lot more powerful than making life beautiful. This was the case in the past and it will remain so in the future. Buildings can play an important role in the necessary shift in our imaginaries and values.

What are the major obstacles?

AP   There are many. First, there are intellectual obstacles. Most of the time, we don't really know what we are talking about when we calculate carbon footprints or do life cycle assessments because we don't know what the boundaries are. Where do we stop? There are some rather fundamental uncertainties with respect to these calculations (what we take into consideration and what we don't, where grey energy is, etc.). These things aren't quite clear, which means we're still having meta-physical debates to determine whether towers are sustainable or not. I haven't read anything decisive on the subject yet. So, if we aren't even capable of figuring out if a skyscraper is good or bad, I think we still have some serious problems to solve from a scientific perspective.

Then, there are problems related to materials and techniques. It's striking how we live in an era of glue (pretty much everything is being stuck instead of nailed and bolted), and how we're more and more dependent on composite materials, though they're difficult to recycle. In practice, we do the exact opposite of what we believe to be good practice—simply because it's cheaper!

We also lack resources, be it knowledge or technical resources. We build exemplary projects like BedZED but aren't capable of doing it at a larger scale. I think there's a problem of scaling up.

What role can digital tools play? Will they impact design? Can they help in the transition towards a more sustainable built environment?

AP   I've conducted research on digital tools and have a certain understanding of how they've influenced design. I've been observing this for many years. Digital technology has profoundly impacted the way architects design; it has allowed for the emergence of new forms of cooperation, thus transforming the organization of the entire profession. Vertical hierarchies are gradually making way for more horizontal kinds of networks. The design process has also been accelerated, and designs can now be replicated and used *ad infinitum* thanks to digital formatting. Building Information Modeling (BIM) will definitely continue to develop. This provides us with an opportunity but also poses a big challenge: if architects lose control over BIM, they'll no longer have any authority—or responsibility—as designers. By 2050, who knows, maybe there will be no design form anymore! Perhaps designers will merely be asked to choose between different categories of forms defined by design algorithms…

I'm not sure whether or not digital tools can support a "sustainable revolution." One reason is that people working with digital tools barely speak to people working in sustainability. In architectural teaching, students working with digital and parametric tools rarely truly exchange with people in the sustainability field. They're not the same species, and this is a real problem.

My intuition is that sustainability issues will also have a major impact on the design process because we're going to have to learn to draw differently. But beyond that, I'd say it's obvious that, more than ever, we'll have to design for the long term, the way landscape designers do. When landscape designers plant a tree, they must think that the tree will grow and, one day, have to be replaced. There's a sort of expanding of time in landscape projects that is very different from building projects, which are seen as deliverable products.

It's also obvious that we'll have to increasingly integrate the life cycle, recycling issues, etc. so that design is thought of as a process rather than as about finding coherency between technical specifications. This, once again, goes back to digital tools, which will take on an important role as designing becomes much more complex.

> Do technical solutions exist but aren't being fully (or correctly) exploited?

AP No, everything hasn't been invented yet. However, imagining we'll find a miracle technical solution one day seems ludicrous. There has to be a social desire for change that triggers a kind of virtuous circle. I think we'll only develop the tools we truly need when we really want to apply them. For instance, we'll only start making progress on the carbon footprint issue when we no longer build without seriously asking the question first.

Moreover, some alternatives are still not completely clear. On one hand, the people searching for solutions are rather "neo-Vitruvian," I'd say. The passive, low-tech solutions they promote consist of playing with built volumes, orientation, natural ventilation, etc. to regulate the building's indoor climate. Then you've got supporters of active, high-tech solutions. The debate between the two sides doesn't seem to be settled, so the question remains open. What strikes me is that we have beginnings of solutions to certain problems, but they're headed in different directions. I think the question isn't about low-tech or high-tech—that's too simple. The real question is knowing what to use according to the context.

> Will the architectural expression of buildings change?

AP Some authors have accused the digital revolution of dematerializing architecture. I don't share this point of view. In my opinion, materiality is currently being redefined by digital technology. I'm actually working on developing this idea of a different kind of materiality based on digital technology—what I call a new "regime of materiality" in my latest book, *"La matérialité de l'architecture"* (Picon 2018).

Furthermore, I think the growing interest in building skins and textures has to do with the question of facades and how they exchange with their surroundings, which is becoming an increasingly important question in architecture. In the 19th century, the big question was the skeleton; in the early 21st century, it's about the skin. Architectural expression does change and probably does so as Paul Valéry describes: *"Ce qu'il y a de plus profond en l'homme, c'est la peau*[5]*."*

> Can we expect changes in users' behavior and expectations?

AP Once again, it's hard to tell. Take, for example, something that's fast developing today: the idea of interactive spaces. It's a real trend. However, I'm of the opinion that when your car relentlessly harangues you to put on your seat belt, it gets on your nerves. You don't always feel like being in this kind of environment, like that of intelligent houses. I think we're defined by our contradictions and torn between contradictory desires. For instance, there's a part of us that appreciates the comfort of having rudimentary forms of artificial intelligence that take care of us, so this will probably continue to develop. At the same time, another part of us doesn't really like it. We're developing the same kind of ambivalent feelings toward technology that the Victorian bourgeoisie had toward their domestic servants: they liked being served and didn't want to make their tea themselves but at the same time didn't like being observed by their servants.

Changes also have to take place in our relationship to thermal comfort and our perception of it. We don't want to go back to being cold, but it's true that we'll have to heat less. There's the idea of heating bodies rather than spaces. Being able to heat spaces has been something of a luxury.

In any case, I think we'll move towards increased flexibility in spaces. This seems clear and goes hand in hand with sustainability. We can't pull down everything that's been built.

Who or what are the triggers, the actors of change?

AP As a historian, I believe the social governs technology and not the other way around, even though technology can suddenly open doors that social change rushes through. I think the biggest problem is that our economic and political systems are based on the denial or postponement of sustainability issues to the medium or long term, despite their urgency. This happens because, fundamentally, the population tacitly agrees to it. There's a phenomenon of procrastination at the scale of humanity, with people stuck in their own problems. Many of us (myself included) have the feeling of social and economic hardship, so sustainability isn't a priority in daily life. We're completely schizophrenic: on one hand, we preach about sustainability, but still travel by plane!

Yet, the actors we need, such as communities, are already there. They just have to make up their minds about getting involved. My concrete contribution as a professor is to discuss these questions with my students here at Harvard. I endeavour to stimulate their intellectual flexibility and curiosity. As a historian, I don't think architecture students should be taught static recipes, but rather should learn how to evolve. History teaches us that change is constant and that nothing is forever. It clearly provides future architects with references. What's more, it also makes them reflect on the idea of change.

"Technology is the only way we can tackle the sustainability challenge."

Carlo Ratti

Carlo Ratti is head of the Senseable City Lab at the Massachusetts Institute of Technology (MIT) and founding partner of the Carlo Ratti Associati design and innovation firm, based in Torino, Italy, with branches in New York and London. Trained as both an architect and an engineer, he regularly shows his work at international exhibitions.

Interview date and location:
16 May 2017, via Skype,
between Lausanne (EPFL) and Boston

What's your definition of a sustainable built environment in a 2050 perspective?

CR   I think the definition, quite simply, is development that does not jeopardize future generations. This initial definition of development that "meets the needs of the present without compromising the ability of future generations to meet their own needs," which comes from the Brundtland report (United Nations and WCED 1987), is a nice definition that still holds true.

What are the challenges and opportunities?

CR   Today, most professionals tend to approach the built environment with a very fragmented perspective. However, to face the sustainability challenge, we must work at a more systemic level by looking at many aspects of society—from energy to mobility, waste, water and so on. All of those aspects must be addressed, and we have to make sure that the overall sustainability is the sum of sustainability at each individual level.

That said, buildings play a significant role. In some countries, like the United States, for instance, the demand for the construction and operation of buildings represents almost 50% of the total energy consumed ^{Figure A}. This is the case today, but it's quite likely that it will continue to be the case in the future and thus will remain a key factor in making our societies more sustainable. The building sector is therefore very important given the energy it uses. Yet, it is rarely evoked in the discussion surrounding sustainability issues. For me, this represents both a challenge and an opportunity.

What are the main obstacles?
What could some of the levers of change be?

CR   With every change, there is some resistance. This resistance can come from the industry sector, the government, in the form of legislation, etc. I'd say that one of the major obstacles is perhaps cultural: the building industry is one of the least digitized. Ensuring that the Internet of Things ^{Figure B} and smart systems enter the building sector is going to be a challenge from a cultural point of view. In the same way that architecture opened up to structural engineering and reinforced concrete constructions in the early 20th century, for instance, today's architecture must open to new, technology-related disciplines, and that requires some effort.

I think technology is going to be a fundamental lever for achieving greater sustainability in the built environment. We have to make our buildings more responsive and capable of saving energy. I think technology is the only way we can tackle the sustainability challenge. Sustainability is about the world of the artificial, as Herbert Simon[6] would call it. So, if you want to change the world of the artificial, it's inherently a technological problem.

Technology will also allow for the necessary changes in occupants' behavior and expectations. Indeed, I believe behavioral

---

[6]   Herbert Simon was an economist and operations researcher with interests and contributions in many fields, including artificial intelligence and decision-making. https://www.informs.org/content/view/full/271830; https://monoskop.org/images/9/9c/Simon_Herbert_A_The_Sciences_of_the_Artificial_3rd_ed.pdf

change is crucial. For that to happen, people must have more knowledge about how buildings operate, how much energy they consume, etc. Usually, behavioral change takes place when we know more about the environment we live in. Again, the Internet of Things is very important in buildings for ensuring that we collect and share the right data with people, who can then enact behavioral change.

> Are there other resources that can help buildings become more sustainable?

CR If we continue to make buildings the way we always have, they're not going to become more sustainable by themselves. So, I think it's all about technology. Technology should be used to save energy in the making of buildings, to produce more sustainable materials and reduce their embodied energy, to run buildings more efficiently using the Internet of Things, to make buildings more responsive and, finally, to encourage behavioral change—which, again, requires technology. Behavioral change starts when we can quantify things. It's very difficult to tell people not to do something unless you can show them the data.

If you consider this across the spectrum—from the construction of the building to the materials used for its operation to occupant behavior—the way you can enable change in all those dimensions is through new technology. I don't see how you can change any of them if we go back to old technology.

> Can you give us examples of how you use digital technology in your work?

CR My firm, Carlo Ratti Associati, recently completed the Agnelli Foundation headquarters in Turin (Italy), for which we used the Internet of Things to create a responsive, digitally-augmented building that can adapt to users' needs in real time ^{Figure C}. We developed a personalized heating, cooling and lighting system with sensors that monitor things like occupants' location, the temperature and the CO_2 concentration. The system "follows" the people inside the space and can then customize their "environmental bubble" via their smartphone. This results in a workplace that naturally learns and is in sync with its occupants' needs. As we don't have to air condition the whole building, a lot of space and energy can be saved.

The other two projects were developed at the Senseable City Lab, which I founded at the Massachusetts Institute of Technology (MIT). The first, the Treepedia project, aims to better quantify the green canopy cover in cities ^{Figure D}. As one of the main strategies for reducing urban temperatures by blocking shortwave radiation and increasing water evaporation, increasing the green canopy in cities is extremely important. Trees not only create more comfortable urban microclimates, but also mitigate air pollution and help avoid flooding during heavy rains thanks to their absorptive root systems. Rather than count

"Behavioral change starts when we can quantify things."

A   Energy consumption per sector in the USA, 2012

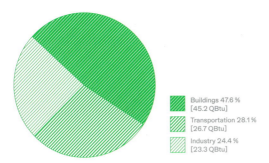

Buildings 47.6 %
[45.2 QBtu]
Transportation 28.1 %
[26.7 QBtu]
Industry 24.4 %
[23.3 QBtu]

B   The Internet of Things:
From connecting devices to human value.

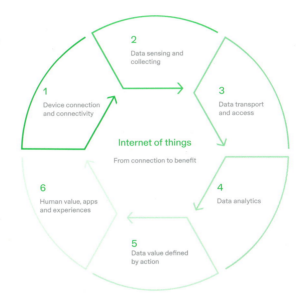

1   **Device Connection**
IoT devices
IoT connectivity
Embedded intelligence

2   **Data sensing**
Capture data
Sensors and tags
Storage

3   **Communication**
Focus on access
Networks, cloud, edge
Data transport

4   **Data analytics**
Big data analysis
AI and cognitive
Analysis at the edge

5   **Data value**
Analysis to action
APIs and processes
Actionable intelligence

6   **Human value**
Smart applications
Stakeholder benefits
Tangible benefits

trees individually, we used data from Google Street View and artificial intelligence to develop a scalable, universally applicable method by analyzing the amount of green perceived while walking down the street. We've also developed a metric called the Green View Index, which quantifies and compares the percentage of tree canopy coverage in a given location. Our database now contains multiple cities that can be compared using our interactive website[7]. We'll continue to add to this database to include cities all over the world.

7 http://senseable.mit.edu/treepedia

The Light Traffic project ^{Figure E}, developed in collaboration with the Swiss Institute of Technology (ETHZ) and the Italian National Research Council (CNR), focuses on self-driving, or autonomous cars. New opportunities emerge when the human brain is replaced by artificial intelligence. We imagined streets where cars could drive faster, closer and more safely and developed slot-based intersections to replace traditional traffic lights, a 150 year-old technology originally designed for horse carriages. Sensor-laden vehicles pass through intersections, can communicate with one another and remain at a safe distance. The advantages are significant: no more stopping at traffic lights, reduced queues and delays cut to almost zero. It was estimated that traffic efficiency could be doubled compared to the current situation.

Finally, a most recent project is the Dynamic Street project ^{Figure F}, developed by Carlo Ratti Associati in collaboration with Alphabet's Sidewalk Labs in Toronto. Here again, self-driving vehicles are at the heart of this urban experiment. We asked ourselves: "How can we make streets reconfigurable, safer and more accessible to pedestrians, cyclists and tomorrow's autonomous vehicles?" We developed a prototype for a modular paving system, which works towards seamlessly adapting the streetscape according to people's needs. For instance, wouldn't it be nice to create an extra car lane during rush hour, but then to turn it into a pedestrian-only plaza in the evening? This added flexibility would have fantastic effects on the quality of the public space by creating the possibility of multiplying and intensifying uses. The project's materiality is based on a series of hexagonal modular pavers that can be easily picked up and replaced—in hours or even minutes—to quickly change the configuration and function of the street without creating disruption.

> In addition to increased technology in buildings, do you think the architectural expression of buildings will change in the future?

CR The first automobiles pretty much looked like carts— with an engine. It took a while for people to realize that there could be more freedom in the design. I can imagine something similar for buildings; you could still design something that looks like a 20th century building, but that works in a different way. It's going to be a pleasant challenge—though not a necessary one—but

C Agnelli Foundation Headquarters, Torino (Italy)
   Carlo Ratto Associati arch., 2017

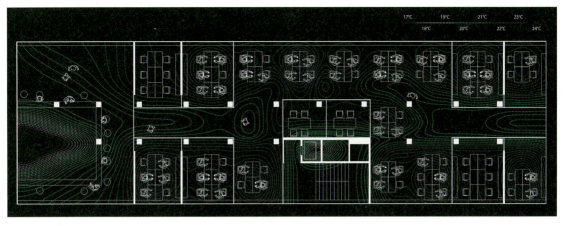

D Treepedia project – Exploring the Green Canopy in cities around the world
   MIT Senseable City Lab, 2015.

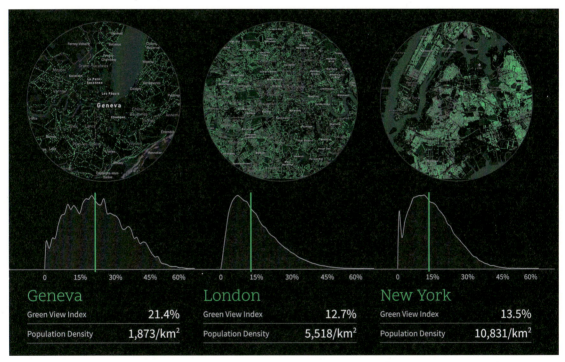

E Light Traffic Project – Revisiting Street Intersections using Slot-Based Systems
MIT Senseable City Lab, 2016

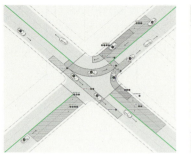 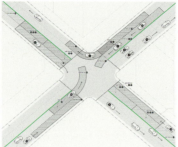 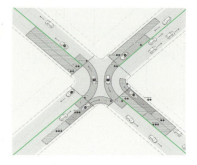

F The Dynamic Street, Toronto (Canada)
Carlo Ratto Associati arch., 2018

> "Many people, including myself, will explore how to create a new register for architectural expression."

many people, including myself, will explore how to create a new register for architectural expression.

Will the design process and actors involved change?

CR I think the design process is changing. If you look at architecture at the time of Palladio, let's say, the skills he talks about in his treatise of architecture deal with the physical world. Then, if you consider architecture in the 20th century, as it changed with the modern movement—Le Corbusier and many others—it became much more technical. Architects had to know how to work with concrete, which then became part of the expression.

Today, changes are heading in the direction we were talking about, meaning more digital technology infused in the physical space. If that's the direction, then you need many more skills at the table. I see the design process becoming much more interdisciplinary, and hence more collaborative.

In this perspective, roles are going to change and new professions will be needed. As architects have usually played a co-ordinating role, they will need to become more familiar with digital technologies. This means changing the curriculum! This is precisely what we are seeing here at MIT: today, most graduating architects know how to programme. That wasn't the case ten years ago, but it's becoming an increasingly widespread global phenomenon. If architects can learn the basics of programming, then they can continue to be the ones to coordinate the process.

"The best way to measure thermal comfort is to ask somebody if they are comfortable, not to measure it."

Koen Steemers

Koen Steemers is currently a professor of Sustainable Design at Cambridge University, where he obtained a PhD in Architecture in 1992. Author of seminal books on topics including daylight design and energy and environmental issues in architecture, his latest research concerns health and well-being in architecture and urban design.

Interview date and location:
27 February 2017, Cambridge, Cambridge University

What is your definition of sustainability?

KS   I received the title "Professor of Sustainable Design" some years ago. It was still a relatively novel term then but has since become commonplace. I'd say my definition has evolved as my research has developed. I started my research career looking primarily at energy efficiency of buildings and carbon-related emissions. It was then that I became acutely aware that the built environment's performance had to do with questions of human expectations. Consequently, human-centric issues became more prominent. This became obvious to our team when we started looking at identical buildings with very different energy performances. Thus, what is critical is understanding how people perceive their environment and how they behave in it.

For instance, we analyzed people's expectations with regard to thermal comfort and the influence of household structure to try to understand why buildings performed the way they did. We found that certain buildings consumed six to ten times more than other, identical buildings. The explanation is simple. A single person who works in London, leaves his/her house at 7 am with everything switched off, comes back at 10 pm, has a microwave meal and goes to bed may live in one of the buildings. In the neighbouring house, however, there could be a family with two children, a dog and one of the parents who works from home and sometimes leaves the backdoor open for the dog with the heating on. Thus, the second home consumes a lot more energy than the first.

It's simple to explain, but we didn't really know how to determine the resilience of one building versus another. If you change the design, what should you change? What should you design for if you want to improve the performance for both types of households? How can you develop a more robust solution?

From those areas of interest I've more recently taken an interest in health and well-being. How does the design of a house create opportunities for social interactions both inside the home and with neighbours? Can a neighbourhood's layout encourage or hinder certain healthy, social relations at different stages of life through features like access to green spaces, particularly considering ageing demographics?

Coming back to the definition of sustainability, it makes sense to talk not only about environmental sustainability but also socio-cultural and economic sustainability. Where exactly health fits in is initially a bit unclear, but it is probably the link between the environmental and the social performance of design. That's the first step: clarifying what we mean by socio-cultural sustainability and environmental sustainability. Achieving one without the other is somewhat pointless. There's no point in achieving environmental sustainability—let's say a zero-carbon society—if the society is dysfunctional socially or economically.

"There's no point in achieving environmental sustainability if the society is dysfunctional socially or economically."

Do you foresee changes in cities and buildings in line with this holistic conception of sustainability between now and 2050?

KS It's an interesting question because it depends where you are. For example, here we are in this building in Cambridge, which is 150 or 200 years old. It's been a home, and now it's an architecture school. Other similar houses nearby have become dental clinics, shops, offices, etc. They could undoubtedly be more environmentally sustainable, but the fact that they're still here, that we're still using all the embodied energy that was put into the building 150 to 200 years ago is a good thing. Our existing buildings have been very resilient and adaptable to change with relatively little intervention. Similarly, at an urban level, if you look at the layers of a city over time and go back hundreds of years, the basic physical structure of a city centre like Cambridge is very much the same; it hasn't changed. From that perspective, 2050 is a very short time period with respect to the built environment.

I think—in the United Kingdom and probably elsewhere in Europe—that one of the major challenges is designing more successful, diverse models of living for an ageing population, which is likely to change the way we design housing. That's not to say that we'll just put all the old people in one place the way we seem to do now, which I don't think is very successful. It simply means that we can design housing in the future to have a longer life cycle in terms of how it's used for different generations and, once again, to be more adaptable. Nowadays, there are old people living in family homes that are often poorly insulated, have a relatively large amount of floor space per person and use a great deal of energy for heating. At the same time, household size (the number of people per house) is becoming smaller while individuals' expectations of comfort and disposable incomes are increasing (a 40% increase since 1990). This results in larger homes (more floor area per person) with more appliances. So, we can certainly observe this phenomenon of greater energy consumption per person than ever before.

All of the improvements in our building regulations have barely caught up with this societal change, in part because we are only building 1–2% of new homes each year, meaning that the 98% of homes don't change. In Western countries, we'll probably have built a relatively small proportion of new buildings compared to the total existing housing stock, maybe 25%, by 2050, leaving us with about 75% of the old building stock ^{Figure A}. So, not only do we need to focus on refurbishment strategies, but we also need to ensure the existing building stock can adapt to new technologies that allow us to work, move and interact in different ways, to new environmental standards and to new comfort requirements. There will be changes in the way we live and work, but perhaps not so much in terms of physical structures.

"There will be changes in the way we live and work, but perhaps not so much in terms of physical structures."

You've conducted several studies on refurbishment. Can you tell us more about urban renewal processes and their relevance for the future?

KS   Some would say we should knock down all the buildings that aren't energy efficient and build brand-new, highly efficient ones. However, that doesn't take into account the life cycle, social fabric and cultural value of the infrastructure. In fact, analyses show that it's better to refurbish old buildings and make them more environmentally sustainable than to knock them down and build new ones, not only for scientific or technical performance reasons, but for these reasons as well ^{Figure B}. I remember having a discussion with a big company in Cambridge. They had two million pounds to invest in their campus, so they asked a group of experts how best to spend the money to improve their environmental performance. Some suggested installing photovoltaic systems on the roof, others a combined heat and power system, others improving the fabric of their buildings, etc. My suggestion was to give the money to the neighbouring housing estates to insulate their old building stock. That would have reduced emissions by a lot more … but of course nobody liked that proposal!

If you want to make a community more sustainable, you have to tackle the poorest buildings and poorest segments of society first, because you can make a big difference in those homes in terms of environmental standards and individuals' health. I think this is achievable within thirty-five years. Certainly more achievable than rebuilding everything and creating "ideal" solutions for 2050, which probably won't be so ideal by 2055 or 2060.

Do you think the design process is likely to change?

> "The way we design needs to be much more interdisciplinary."

KS   Indeed, the way we design needs to be much more interdisciplinary. We're no longer designing conventional office spaces; we're designing office spaces that are also leisure spaces: part home, part café and part gym. The idea of having an office design specialist is almost contradictory to where things seem to be going, unless you think offices are special in themselves.
In the old days, you might have designed an office space for 100 people. Today, you'd design that same office for fifty people because you know fifty employees will be out and about working from home or with clients, on the road, in planes or in cafés. These different ways of working and the opportunities for not working in a physical office space that digital technology affords mean that the demands and the way of developing work scenarios are quite different from what they were thirty or forty years ago.

Let's consider another example. We did a lot of work on outdoor comfort some time back and found that the most important indicator of whether somebody is comfortable outdoors is whether they choose to be there or not. If they're waiting for a bus and it's cold and windy, they hate it. If they're chatting with friends,

A Evolution of the building stock, 2010–2050

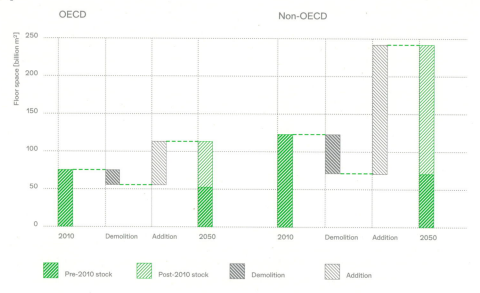

OECD   Non-OECD

Pre-2010 stock   Post-2010 stock   Demolition   Addition

B Benefits of renovation for different actors

Environmental benefits	Economic benefits	Social benefits
• Energy savings & GHG emissions reduction • Reduced usage of materials	• Employment • GDP and public budgets • Innovation • Sectoral modernisation • Energy Security • Productivity benefits	• Health benefits • Reduction energy poverty • Wellbeing / Comfort benefits • Energy bill savings • Increase in property value & tenant satisfaction

they feel perfectly good in the same climatic conditions and wearing the same clothes. What determines their comfort is purely psychological. I think the same thing will happen in our future designs: we'll be much more interested in understanding the interconnectedness between social and environmental aspects. Environmental sustainability criteria are only a small part of the opportunities and challenges, and must be understood in terms of how people like to live and work, the freedom of choice they want and how this freedom influences their perception of happiness and comfort.

Will the role of architects change as well?

KS   I think that depends very much on what country you're in. In certain countries, architects still have a traditional status. This isn't the case in the UK because the profession has become more limited in terms of the skills required. For example, when I started doing consultancy and practice, I was doing daylight calculations. Few engineers could do daylight analysis twenty years ago because they weren't taught how. It wasn't part of their curriculum. Nowadays, I imagine most engineers can do daylight analysis as part of their normal environmental consultancy. They can do passive design analysis as well as mechanical services. There's been a shift. Environmental and services engineers do much of the work architects once did, but they don't necessarily combine those skills with design skills and so don't think of daylight as an aesthetic concern. At the other end of the design spectrum, architects have handed site management tasks over to specialists (contracts consultants, for instance).

So, the architectural profession has been squeezed from both the delivery side and the design side. However, it has also identified new ways of working and new channels for using architectural skills in the broader built environment. In the United Kingdom, there's certainly been a shift or rather a widening of the role architects play. I think this is crucial because, often, architects do not question whether they improve their projects in sustainability terms. They get a commission to design a luxury house or a prestigious office and do it. However, examples do exist of how the architect or design team can interact with their client and understand their needs to provide a better design or more sustainable scenario.

Are these changes reflected in the education architects receive?

KS   Changes are definitely taking place in the way we teach architecture. Of course, we're teaching them more about energy efficiency. However, by the time they start practicing, there is a risk that what they're learning now will already be outdated, as things are changing so quickly. What I'm teaching them about now is health and well-being, which are going to be important issues when they begin practicing. More importantly, we train our

> "We train our architecture students to be critical, imaginative, creative thinkers."

architecture students to be critical, imaginative, creative thinkers so they can respond to the pressures and challenges they'll face long after they've completed their education.

This new teaching approach is starting to have a concrete impact, and we're starting to see new kinds of practices. A group of students from this department, for instance, has created the Assemble architecture collective, a kind of bottom-up cooperative design group that goes into a community and lives and works with it in order to re-design the neighbourhood ^{Figure C}. Part of what this new way of working does is to reveal to clients what is possible, and what the policy challenges and practical opportunities are. The other part is actually physically building things and acting on the fabric of the neighbourhood itself. Typically work might involve co-design or cooperative scenarios wherein the community plays the key role. The aim is demonstrating how our impact as architects can be much more creative. This approach is not explicitly and outwardly sustainable. It's not about installing photovoltaics or doubling the insulation. It's about reusing what we have at an architectural scale.

What about the role of technology?

KS   I think there are two things technology, for example smart phones, can do. For one, they're a good way of allowing users to know what's going on in their environment. For example, a phone could tell its owner: "Do you realise you are walking through a really polluted environment right now? But if you turn right and go along this green route, you won't be exposed to it, you'll be more comfortable and it won't take you more than a minute longer to get to where you're going." It would serve as a map to propose users healthier routes, provide information about the quality of the environment and give them choices about how to use this information. Secondly, we can obtain an enormous amount of data from mobile technologies. We can find out where people are, what they're exposed to, how much energy they consume and how physically active they are. This notion of wearable technology could really become a useful resource for understanding exposure to various things in our environment, pollution being an obvious example.

Then there's all of the sensor technology that can be embedded in buildings to record their performances, such as fluctuations in temperature, or to determine whether the physical structure needs repairing, etc. In terms of building control and maintenance, embedded sensing seems extremely useful. That technology could also be used to communicate with people's personal mobile equipment (i.e. wearables).

However, the best way to measure thermal comfort is to ask somebody if they are comfortable, not to measure it. A measurement doesn't tell you whether you're comfortable or not; it just tells you what the temperature is. So the combination of the

C Yardhouse, Sugarhouse Studios, Stratford (United Kingdom)
Assemble arch., 2014

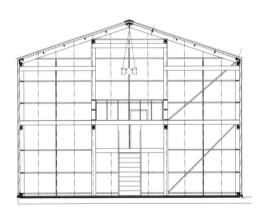
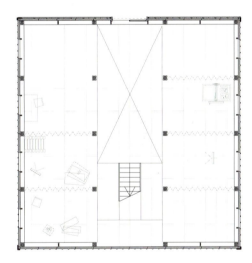

two (measurement and survey) can be very powerful. If you have all the measurements and you see how people respond to those measurements, you can observe how their reactions to questions regarding their comfort may differ. The thermal environment may be identical, but the responses may vary depending on simple things. If I cycle to work, I'll be hot and I'll want to open windows in my office. Somebody who drives will feel cooler and will complain if I open the windows. Thus, two people in the same physical environment can have very different perceptions of thermal comfort. There is increasing emphasis on occupant surveys and questionnaires in buildings, particularly regarding the issue of health and well-being.

I've always been very interested in diversity and creating designs that allow people to find their place. Instead of having everybody designing in a way so as to maximize the benefits, we should be designing from one extreme to another, from one range to another, so that everybody can find their place, their space and the conditions that best suit them. That's a much richer way of thinking about the built environment than trying to optimize it. If you try to optimize, you're designing for the average person, and there's nobody who's average. Nobody says, "I'm average." There's no "optimum" to design for today, and there will definitely no "optimum" fifty years from now, when we really don't know what's going to happen or how people will be living. Diversity, on the other hand, can trigger social interactions and help build a kind of social resilience that can be beneficial in the fight against climate change.

Do you think the expression of buildings will change?

KS In terms of architectural expression, I worry about the imposing of energy-driven design strategies. We saw this in the 1970s with the energy crisis. All the innovative new houses built during that period were designed to be zero or near-zero energy, and they were horrible. They were like energy-generating machines, not places to live that people could call home.

However, in theory, if you combine sensing technologies, adaptive technologies for building facades and perhaps the parametric modeling being used in certain architecture labs, extraordinary building forms can be generated. It seems to me that, for now, these technologies are used purely aesthetically and rarely for true performance or sustainability goals. However, if you can combine these technologies and actually use architectural parametric modeling to create a building that performs differently depending on the occupant, the season, interior functions, internal gains, etc., then you can imagine a building that's adaptable and adjustable to various conditions. Whether that alone can create appropriate architecture for our streets and cities, I don't know. It might make a great prototype as an exhibi-

"If you try to optimize, you're designing for the average person, and there's nobody who's average."

tion building. This goes back to the problem I mentioned earlier of whether this approach creates good cities and spaces or is just a fashion.

What are the key drivers of a more sustainable built environment?

KS	What is probably going to spark change is a series of problems or disasters. That's likely to generate the fastest responses. It's like back in the 1980s when we got rid of CFCs. When people made the connection between the hole in the ozone layer and the use of hairspray and refrigeration, they boycotted those industries, which consequently suddenly took an interest and changed. CFCs were quickly banned. Implementing the policy was easy because the population agreed and the industry had to make changes if it wanted to survive economically.

The discovery of the hole in the ozone layer was a very specific problem directly associated with CFCs. There was an obvious solution— get rid of them. When we talk about sustainability issues or global warming in general, there are so many interconnected parameters and variables that it's difficult to pinpoint one particular act that's going to make a specific difference. There are so many consequences and causes and they're all linked, which makes it very difficult to draw the line and make a direct connection.

I sometimes wonder whether we architects and built-environment specialists actually have sufficient will to make much of an impact. Yet, we all must play a role and provide solutions to these problems. What's hard for architects is anticipating how they might influence change in a broader way. What I mean here is that even a highly sustainable design still rarely has a net positive benefit, which is the goal for truly sustainable design.

People often say that policy is a driver, and that building regulations will force everyone to be more energy-efficient. To my mind, however, building regulations have always been the minimum standard that developers and builders can get away with. It's not the best we can do; it's really more of a bottom line than the leading edge. If you look at the entire building stock, then we could agree that changing building regulations every time somebody builds a new building and stepping them up in terms of energy efficiency is definitely a good bottom-up driver. However, building regulations are very much influenced by the industry, so there's a lot of resistance from the industry to make a radical change.

One positive achievement in terms of building regulations is that, in the past ten years or so, we've started telling the industry where building regulations will be five years from now; for example, what the (lower) U-value will need to be, etc. Builders can see it coming and can start preparing for it by ramping up skills, looking for material options and developing construction scenarios. That kind of anticipation has been effective.

"What is probably going to spark change is a series of problems or disasters. That's likely to generate the fastest responses."

Three success factors for buildings in 2050

Tatiana Bilbao

1 A building should be diverse and inclusive for many different types of people.

2 A building should offer communities the possibility to express themselves.

3 A building should promote a responsible way of inhabiting the world.

Paula Cadima

1. The most adaptable possible for the people who are going to inhabit it, but also bearing in mind that these people will not be there forever, and that new users may have different lifestyles.

2. Flexible.

3. Recyclable.

Lionel Devlieger

1. The building should be adaptable.

2. The building should be designed for deconstruction so that its materials can still be reused even after it has disappeared. A kind of resource repository.

3. Above all, it should be supported by a thriving, lively economy that can keep the promises embedded in that building. There's no point in having ambitions for a building that is disassemblable if there's no economy around it (e.g. operators who are willing and able to dismantle it and recycle its components).

Herbert Girardet

1 Being clean environmentally speaking. A building that doesn't need power from some power station hundreds of miles away to keep it going.

2 It can also supply energy (for example, to other buildings), via integrated battery storage.

3 Conviviality. A building should be convivial and not machine-like. It should also be interesting in terms of stimuli. Eco-design tends to be very stern and quite technical. We need to move away from that.

Alistair Guthrie

1. The building has to be integrated into the city or town or wherever it's located. That means the surroundings (the built environment as a whole) are as important as the building itself.

2. The building should be designed based on the idea of a circular economy, which means we have to think not only about the building itself, but also about the community as a whole.

3. Different technologies, which are still in the labs today, should be applied to different building elements (material use and recycling, new ways of using resources, etc.).

Kengo Kuma

1. Buildings in 2050 should be self-made systems. Everyone should be able to make their own home using their own hands.

2. Buildings in 2050 should be soft. Materials should evoke weaving, like fabric or cloth.

3. Buildings in 2050 should be flexible. A good example of this is traditional Japanese houses, where the walls and windows can easily be moved or removed.

Ali Malkawi

1 A building that can respond to its surroundings and engage its users, since we spend most of our time in buildings and feel happier in an aesthetically pleasing, healthy environment.

2 A building that can act as a positive agent in that particular site (its environment) by actually improving it.

3 A building that needs minimal resources to operate and ideally produces more than it uses.

So, contributing in terms of adding (positive impact) and eliminating (e.g. removing whatever pollutants might be there). This is definitely possible. The question is, how large of a scale can you reach? You'd hope it's not just certain wealthy countries that can deploy it, but less affluent ones as well.

Edward Ng

1. People must be very happy using it.

2. And people must be very happy using it.

3. Design for the people… everything else is just gimmicks!

   People must be happy using the building in a natural and efficient way, without having to turn devices on or waste a lot of energy.

Susan Parnell

1 First, if the money that had been spent on it between now and then were spent on maintenance rather than reconstruction.

2 Secondly, it should be appreciated by many types of people. For instance, people who only walk past it on their way to work each day because it has a beautiful exterior but have never been inside, people who go to work in it each day and people who visit it for special occasions.

3 It gives more than it has takes, following the concept of the building as an ecological and social multiplier.

Antoine Picon

For me, Vitruvius' triad is more relevant than ever:

1. A building should be constructed and function in such a way as to contribute positively to the evolution of its environment (*firmitas*, solidity).

2. A building should propose uses that are in line with the new values and lifestyles of a society that is slightly more austere (*utilitas*, commodity).

3. A building should offer luxury and sumptuousness (*venustas*, beauty).

Carlo Ratti

1. Sustainability.

2. Sociability, because buildings will play a bigger role in bringing us together, especially office buildings. Working is becoming an increasingly social activity.

3. Sensuality, in the sense that buildings should be expressions of sociability and sustainability in their physical form.

Koen Steemers

1. Adaptable. A building that can take advantage of opportunities and changing conditions (climate, behaviors, needs). Adaptable means it doesn't have to be knocked down and rebuilt.

2. Diverse. Diverse means that we should create different kinds of environments that suit people in different stages of their lives or days. In some ways, it's the opposite of optimizing.

3. Integrated. Integration means a building that positively enhances its environment and contributes to urban life or socio-cultural activities in its surroundings, for the good of humankind.

Re-thinking sustainability

Sophie Lufkin
Emilie Nault
Marilyne Andersen
Emmanuel Rey

Before reflecting on the potential implications of these twelve interviews regarding the future *smart living lab* building, we would like to come back to the overall approach used in this book. If there were any doubts on the usefulness—or, rather, the necessity—of exploring possible futures, the insights offered by this series of prospects should contribute to offset them. Any attempt at making accurate predictions would be a futile and counterproductive enterprise given the complexity of the issues at stake; instead, this overview seeks to open up fresh, insightful perspectives on multiple possible futures, which resonate with the interviewees' diverse cultural backgrounds and disciplines. In so doing, it also brings nuances to some of the concerns that underlie the numerous reports and studies on future projections and scenarios. Moreover, spreading awareness about the nature of these current trends may help alter them (Barney 1993) and encourage learning, reflection and personal choice (Meadows, Randers, and Meadows 2004).

By comparing the opinions of internationally-renowned experts in different fields related to the built environment—not only with each other but also with the past and possible future trends scattered throughout this manuscript—we hope to contribute to the ubiquitous discussion of the future in a complementary way. The confluence of these twelve open discussions with practitioners was an opportunity to sketch out paths and perspectives for architectural design for 2050. This notion of future projection is intrinsic to architectural design itself; every project expresses the desire to change the present of a place in a more or less explicit way and to create new conditions for a duration that is—admittedly—undetermined, but likely to outlive its designers. In terms of sustainability transitions, the interactions between knowledge regarding the notions of space and of time will undeniably play a growing and essential role.

Interestingly enough, and despite varied and contrasting expert horizons, several opinions converge. For one, there is a clear consensus that the notion of sustainability itself is a founding concept that has played an essential role in the search for new long-term equilibria, but that appears to be no longer sufficient to address the multiple challenges for 2050. On one hand, as Girardet points out, "sustain is a very passive term." On the other hand, many experts note that environmental aspects tend to be prioritized at the expense of socio-cultural and/or economic sustainability (Parnell, Girardet, Cadima) or, more critically, to the detriment of other related dimensions such as health or culture (Steemers, Malkawi). In reaction, while some experts—like Devlieger for instance—challenge the concept of sustainability, others advocate for a shift towards an amped-up version: a "sustainability+" concept for Parnell, a "regenerative built environment" for Girardet and "smart cities" for Picon.

A Generate favorable framework conditions

1 Rebalance economic systems

2 Implement proactive public policies

3 Empower communities

4 Develop circular dynamics

We like to consider this "enhanced" sustainability concept, which echoes the idea of multiple sustainability transitions, as an invitation to rethink the very notion of sustainability and to adopt a revisited, expanded vision of the concept. It is a call to tread the middle path between inert pessimism and boundless optimism. In this spirit, the interviews can be used as raw material from which to identify a series of priority actions. These pathways represent the most basic, most fundamental variables for architectural design in a 2050 perspective. They can be structured according to three main axes, which we defined in terms of proactive dynamics:

A   Generate favourable framework conditions
This axis, which corresponds to the first section of our interview guide, refers to global, contextual issues for the built environment as a whole, i.e. in a systemic perspective. Looking ahead to 2050, what are the major challenges and opportunities for creating more favourable framework conditions for enhanced sustainability transitions?

1   Rebalance economic systems
Be it for the Global North or the Global South, most experts more or less explicitly agree that the first condition to enable true sustainability transitions is to reform the current economic system. Costs cannot remain the only driver. In Bilbao's view, "the major obstacle [...] is global capitalism." Along the same line of reasoning, Parnell puts neoliberalism at the top of her list of challenges. Picon feels that the "biggest problem is that our economic and political systems are based on the denial [...] of sustainability issues [...] despite their urgency." Ng stresses how our lifestyles are based "mostly on economic development" and, finally, Kuma argues that the only way to rebuild a solid "relationship to place," as he calls it, is through a major rebalance of the economic system. This re-anchoring of the production of values in better coherence with the territories directly concerned requires not only a strengthening of the endogenous potentials, but also — and undoubtedly — the emergence of a true new economic culture that can better favor and enhance the creation of value chains at the regional scale.

2   Implement proactive public policies
The legal framework appears to be a powerful driver for rebalancing economic systems in the eyes of our experts. Girardet, for instance, calls for "more policies and incentives" as "the market alone cannot solve the problem." Commenting on the energy debate in general and on recycling more specifically, Guthrie declares that "the real changes have come from top-down regulations." Later on in the discussion, he uses the example of photovoltaics to underline how architects "love" constraints, which unlock their creativity

potential. Thus, as other interviewees also suggest, these top-down approaches could potentially play an essential role in the future, both as incentives and deterrents. Parnell calls for the implementation of a positive fiscal framework in the form of "strong tax policies against CO_2." While Devlieger insists on the need for public incentives to stimulate reuse in the building sector, he also emphasises the governments' responsibility in outlawing programmed obsolescence. In the absence of public policies that are more inclusive in terms of sustainability and more proactive in terms of tangible results on the ground, it seems difficult to envisage true sustainability transitions in the next thirty years and to respond to the degree of urgency of these global issues.

3   Empower communities

If top-down approaches are key, bottom-up ones are no less crucial—and complementary. Guthrie is convinced of the importance of these mechanisms, which, he predicts, will be more of a driving force in the future. Bilbao also believes people have the potential to become a resource that is powerful enough to "break the cycles of money and business-oriented dynamics." However, this societal shift will happen only if people's awareness of sustainability issues improves. How to achieve this? With exemplary buildings and exhibitions, answers Picon, which will definitely pave the road towards empowered communities. The accelerated transfer of knowledge to the general public that has been underway since the beginning of the century has clearly exceeded the boundaries of experts in the area of sustainability issues, thus generating a domino effect with multiple relays.

4   Develop circular dynamics

Our expert panel is unanimous on this point: buildings can no longer be considered as isolated entities. Rather, they must be integrated within their urban environment, says Guthrie. Going beyond the concept of dense and compact cities, he makes the case for a circular economy, which he defines as a system wherein "everything used stays in circulation through recycling." With his concept of the "Ecopolis," Girardet also refers to an "ecologically and economically restorative" city. Picon further develops the idea of rethinking "the notion of solidarity between buildings." He claims that new types of synergies that overcome the reductionist "geometric" dimension must be established between buildings. This means that new technologies shall be used to more efficiently manage the relationship between the environment, materials, processes, etc., thus allowing our cities to become "smart." The result is a promising vision of new symbioses in the built environment to intensify the search for more coherent and dynamic interchanges in the relationship between our requirements (what we need) and our resources (what we have).

B Revive architectural design

1 Delight the user
2 Cultivate the potential for adaptability
3 Recycle materials and reuse components
4 Design buildings as multipliers

B   Revive architectural design
         This second axis relates more specifically to the buildings themselves. What role will buildings play with respect to the aforementioned global challenges? Which resources can we activate and what potential can we unleash to revive architectural design?

1   Delight the user
         While sustainability—or its amplified version—is clearly a necessary precondition, it alone is not sufficient. What good is an ultra-efficient, functional building without architectural quality? Conversely, what good is an iconic building with poor environmental performances and/or low potential for appropriation by its users? Throughout the interviews, the idea of (re)connecting architectural quality with sustainability principles stands out as one of the major challenges for the future. As Cadima claims, a sustainable building is one that will "make people happy." Later on, she argues that "sustainability isn't only about energy; it's also about quality." Girardet uses the term "conviviality" versus "machine-like, stern eco-design." For buildings to be appreciated by a great variety of users (Parnell) or, as Bilbao says, to be "inclusive for many different types of people," the first prerequisite is diversity. Architects' must therefore resist cost-driven monotony (Kuma) and propose unique, context-specific solutions that, though potentially more risky (Cadima), will lead to "greater spatial, programmatic or typological diversity" (Bilbao). For Steemers, this means creating varied designs that will not only "allow people to find their place," but also help create more resilient environments.

2   Cultivate the potential for adaptability
         The current context of accelerated changes and growing uncertainties—regarding the climate, for one, but also our behaviours with respect to living and working environments (more home-based work, fewer office spaces needed, etc.)—calls for buildings capable of adapting to new uses. Virtually all of our experts share this concern for adaptability, albeit with their own personal interpretations of the term. According to Steemers, an adaptable building can not only withstand these changing conditions, but can take advantage of them. This follows Parnell's idea: "Adaptable means it doesn't have to be knocked down and rebuilt" (which, with all things considered, appears to be a sensible condition for sustainability). When Picon predicts that "we'll move towards increased flexibility in spaces," he is mainly focusing on the spatial dimension of flexibility. Devlieger and Cadima add the temporal dimension as well, arguing that a building must be adaptable over time. Though no less concerned about adaptability, Ratti distinguishes himself

by his technology-oriented approach. For example, he uses the Internet of Things to create "digitally-augmented buildings" that respond to users' needs in real time.

3   Recycle materials and reuse components

Promoting the use of reusable materials along with cultivating the potential for adaptability is an efficient strategy for dealing with rapidly changing conditions (Cadima). Picon adeptly pinpoints a major issue here: the fact that we use glue instead of nails because it is cheaper, which makes recycling impossible. However, as Guthrie illustrates with several examples, promising new techniques exist in this area. While most of our experts—regardless of whether they are academics or practitioners—insist on the urge to increase our use of recyclable materials, Devliger's approach is clearly the most radical. According to him, not only should architects "design for deconstruction" so that materials can be reused, but they should also "design using reclaimed components." This latter challenge, which certainly adds a number of constraints to the design process, is systematically absent in the architectural debate. The possible integration of emerging dynamics linked to a circular economy into architectural design will undoubtedly fuel these types of approaches and lines of questioning.

4   Design buildings as multipliers

This last priority action at the building scale is an invitation to consider buildings as "sustainability activators." Each expert insists more or less emphatically on one (or more) sustainability dimension(s) according to his or her background. Parnell, for example, likes to imagine the building of the future not as a consumer, but as an entity that gives more than it takes: a "social, ecological multiplier." For Malkawi, buildings should help improve their environment, both adding to it by acting as a "positive agent" and eliminating from it by removing pollutants. Steemers also develops this idea of a building that positively enhances its community, fosters urban life and supports socio-cultural activities. While Girardet and Guthrie emphasise the environmental dimension, and notably the potential for energy production and storage, Kuma focuses on the economic benefits. He argues that buildings should support the local market and depend first and foremost on local resources—both material-wise and in terms of craftspeople. This fundamental shift, he says, is essential to re-establish what he calls the "relationship to place." By implementing these types of approaches in an environment that is already largely built, the goal is not to start over from scratch but to target new ways to value existing resources within urban areas while improving their use.

C   Generate new interactions

1 Promote interdisciplinary processes

2 Support evaluative approaches

3 Reconnect design with users aspirations

4 Adapt the education of future architects

C   Generate new interactions
This third and final axis focuses on stakeholders and processes. Who are the key stakeholders and how should they further commit to initiating change and making the paradigm shifts mentioned above a reality? What direction must practices move toward so as to generate new interactions that will re-establish connections within fragmented processes?

1   Promote interdisciplinary processes
For the twelve interviewees, architectural design that is completely self-absorbed and disconnected from other related disciplines is not a viable solution for dealing with the complexity of these issues. Devlieger points to an exaggerated "architectural ego" that creates this disconnect between designers and experts from other backgrounds. Bridging this gap in the design process is widely acknowledged as a major challenge for the decades to come, due on one hand to a certain resistance within the discipline, but also—and in large part—to a highly conservative construction sector, explains Kuma. With a broad interdisciplinary experience, Guthrie is also an ardent defender of integrated design. He is convinced that "All the best, most sustainable projects are the result of collaboration between different experts." As far as our societies in transformation go and the growing complexity that results from this, Steemers argues that "the way we design needs to be much more interdisciplinary" if we want to succeed in designing spaces that are adapted to emerging and unconventional lifestyles. Ratti is equally clear regarding the importance of interdisciplinarity, but for slightly different reasons. According to him, the increasing presence of "digital technology infused in the physical space" requires more skills, and will thus automatically lead to more collaborative processes. Yet, it is important not to lose sight of the need for conceptual and spatial coherence in architectural design. While this dimension remains central for the quality of any project, enhancing this with more integrative dynamics starting from the conceptual phase seems crucial.

2   Support evaluative approaches
The second factor of disconnection that must be addressed is the gap between practice and research. According to our experts, evaluation-based approaches are still largely missing from professional practice. Yet, concerted efforts should be made to help them become an integral part of the design process, both prior to and upon completion of projects. On the one hand, life cycle assessments (LCA) during the early design stages are a recurrent theme in the discussions. Guthrie feels strongly that making LCA manda-

tory will incite people to think more about the origin of materials and make more conscious decisions. He and many others believe that providing people with information is a fundamental lever for change. Post-occupancy studies are another effective way to learn from buildings and avoid making the same mistakes. Two not necessarily exclusive visions emerge on this topic. For some, including Cadima, Ratti, Malkawi and Guthrie, among others, monitoring necessitates technology: "sensors, connected to computational tools as well as artificial intelligence" (Malkawi). For others, like Ng and Kuma, visiting the building to gather feedback from occupants is an important, simple, inexpensive way to supplement the information collected from the sensors. Steemers has similar feelings: "The best way to measure thermal comfort is to ask somebody if they are comfortable, not to measure it." This search for quantitative and/or qualitative assessments of built areas is a call to improve knowledge about building life and capitalize on new insights for future projects.

3   Reconnect design with users' aspirations
The third fragmentation applies to the relationship between architects and occupants. The majority of experts acknowledge the ongoing lack of coordination between building conception and usage, which often leads to occupants' dissatisfaction and/or misuse of the building. Thus, rebuilding the relationship between the architectural design and its future user is key. Three different degrees of interpretation can be highlighted. First, the more basic idea of "designing for the people," the goal of which is to create spaces that suit occupants' needs. Second, "designing with the people," i.e. directly integrating the user in the design process so that "the built object is truly the result of these rich interactions" (Bilbao). These participative processes are, of course, more demanding, especially when the future user is not the client. Third, "designing for self-construction," certainly the most radical expression of the desire to make building users become the focus, and thus applicable in specific contexts only, as expressed by Kuma.

4   Adapt the education of future architects
The idea of an architectural education reform also produced a consensus among many of the interviewees and was clearly perceived as a powerful lever for action. Cadima, for instance, cites education as a primary driver of change. So what, then, should we reform? Two potential paths emerge. To begin with, most experts condemn the separation between design and engineering in the architecture curriculum (as in professional practice) and call for more interdisciplinary education. Second, though less strongly, many—more notably academics– insist on the need to heighten future architects' awareness of evaluation-based approaches (LCA, post-occupancy studies) by addressing these topics in their

teaching. As one might expect, each expert also expresses his or her desire for a better integration of their own central priority. Ng, for example, endeavours to help students rediscover simplicity and fundamental, natural laws. "Come back to the basics," he says. Parnell suggests "adapt[ing] curriculums so as to build [moral] responsibility" by adding topics such as philosophy and ethics. Devlieger would like students to learn to design using reclaimed components. Ratti, with his strong focus on technology, stresses the importance of teaching the basics of programming to ensure architects' role in coordinating the design process. Finally, Steemers formulates what seems to be a particularly promising lead: with everything changing so quickly and unexpectedly, he says, architecture students should be trained to be critical, imaginative thinkers who deal creatively with future pressures and challenges.

Despite these twelve areas of consensus, one point of contention in particular emerged among the experts: the role of technology, a controversial subject that leaves no one indifferent. Some, like Devlieger, do not necessarily reject technology outright, but express different concerns. For him, the overvaluation of innovation (or claims of innovation) is an unfortunate reality, as is programmed obsolescence. Furthermore, he argues that "All the best examples (…) of efficient resource use in architecture are from the past." At the other extreme, we find Ratti, a staunch supporter of technology. "Technology," he claims, "is the only way we can tackle the sustainability challenge."

A middle road seems to appear between these two radical positions. While it is clear that technology continues its advance and that architecture is inevitably impacted by the development of digital technology, renewable materials and energy management, the quest for more fundamentally sustainable approaches encourages experts to question the validity of certain innovations. In other words, an approach that neither completely rejects nor puts blind faith in technology requires to take a critical perspective, resorting to it when it provides a sensible added value rather than to compensate for design flaws or shortcomings that could have been avoided more convincingly otherwise. Picon's approach perfectly illustrates this stance. "We're still in the gadget phase, where there's never enough technology. However, we'll soon have to exit that phase and enter the actual smart city 'savings mode,' where it's not necessarily good to put sensors everywhere. We'll have to determine what's good and bad usage of technology." Guthrie's approach is similar. "Technology is hugely important," he says "but I don't think it will solve everything."

He's probably right: more technology does not necessarily go hand in hand with more sustainability (Andersen 2017). To fully grasp this, it is important to understand how technology can be applied to buildings. Three distinct dimensions exist:

1) computational tools that can be used during the design process to simulate various parameters,
2) the building's technical installations (heating, ventilation, air conditioning, boiler rooms, refrigeration, fire protection, smoke removal and plumbing), and
3) sensors to regulate (and ideally monitor) the building's performances.

In this sense, while the goal is to avoid an increase in energy-consuming devices (2), the appropriate strategy seems to use technology mainly during the design (1) and post-occupancy phases (3) as a knowledge tool for optimising the relationship between needs and resources. In other words, emphasise intelligence and minimise machinery (Rey 2015). Somewhere between high-tech and low-tech, we could envisage research and solutions aimed at developing "smart low-tech." Such an approach unquestionably opens up a stimulating perspective for future buildings, including the *smart living lab*.

Yet, it would be simplistic to reduce the question of innovation to that of technological progress. The interviews highlight that innovation is also social, cultural, organizational and procedural. In this broader view of the concept of innovation, it appears that a place designed as a platform for innovation for the habitat of the future (i.e. the *smart living lab*) will have to not only leave ample room for technology, but will also have to develop specific thinking to stimulate the quest for inventiveness on multiple scales.

Be that as it may, at the end of this editorial adventure, a few questions nonetheless remain unanswered. For one, how can the outcomes be applied to the Swiss context? What is the relevance of these findings for the *smart living lab* building? The various steps and stages that will mark the design and development of this unique building will provide some answers. A research programme called "Building2050" was dedicated specifically to this process—and its outcomes are presented in the second book of the Towards 2050 series entitled "Exploring. Research-driven Building Design." They have become the basis from which various architectural approaches will emerge for the future *smart living lab* building.

The present book demonstrates that we should not wait for unfortunate events or disasters to occur to start changing things. From a sustainability perspective, the interviews offered to the reader will hopefully provide both deep and broad insights that may encourage actors currently working within the building sector, regardless of their discipline, professional context or means of contribution, to question their own room for manoeuver for the decades to come and to rethink the way certain levers of action can be used, fostered or invented.

References

A

ADEME. 2009. "Les transports électriques en France: un développement nécessaire sous contraintes." *ADEME & Vous – Stratégie & Études,* 352.

Andersen, Marilyne. 2017. "Qualité architecturale et durabilité: de longues fiançailles." *Bilan – Supplément "Habitat"* August 30: 2.

Andersen, Marilyne, and Emmanuel Rey. 2013. "Le projet *smart living lab* à Fribourg: un bâtiment du futur en site réel." *La Vie Economique,* no. 11: 26–26.

Arcadis. 2015. *Sustainable Cities Index 2015. Balancing the Economic, Social and Environmental Needs of the World's Leading Cities.*

Arup Foresight. 2013. *It's Alive! Can You Imagine the Urban Building of the Future?* London: Arup.

B

Ballif, Christophe, Laure-Emmanuelle Perret-Aebi, Sophie Lufkin, and Emmanuel Rey. 2018. "Integrated Thinking for Photovoltaics in Buildings." *Nature Energy* 3: 438–42.

Barney, Gerald O. 1993. *Global 2000 Revisited. What Shall We Do?* Virginia: Millennium Institute.

Berque, Augustin. 1996. *Etre humains sur la Terre.* Paris: Gallimard.

Bolwell, Andrew. 2016. "Megatrends Shaping Our Future." *HP Innovation Journal,* no. 2. https://www8.hp.com/us/en/hp-labs/innovation-journal-issue2/megatrends-shaping-the-future.html.

Bourdeau, Luc. 1996. "Le bâtiment à l'horizon 2030." *Futuribles* 208: 39–61.

Braungart, Michael, and William McDonough. 2009. *Cradle to Cradle. Remaking the Way We Make Things.* New York: Vintage.

Breit, Stefan, and Detlef Gürtler. 2018. *Microliving. Urbanes Wohnen im 21. Jahrhundert.* Zurich: Gottlieb Duttweiler Institute (GDI).

Brice, Lucie, Anne Dujin, and Bruno Maresca. 2012. *Les pratiques de consommation émergentes dans les quartiers durables. Consommations d'énergie et de mobilité.* Vol. C294. Cahiers de recherche CREDOC.

C

CH2011. 2011. *Swiss Climate Change Scenarios CH2011.* Zurich: C2SM, MeteoSwiss, ETH, NCCR Climate, and OcCC. http://www.ch2011.ch/pdf/CH2011reportLOW.pdf.

CH2014-Impacts. 2014. *Toward Quantitative Scenarios of Climate Change Impacts in Switzerland.* Bern: OCCR, FOEN, MeteoSwiss, C2SM, Agroscope and ProClim. http://ch2014-impacts.ch/res/files/CH2014-Impacts_report.pdf.

Cohen, Lorette. 2009. "Nourrir et dépasser le métier d'architecte." *Le Temps,* 17 August 2019: 10.

Communauté des sites de Ressources documentaire pour une Démocratie Mondiale (Coredem). 2013. *Paysages de l'après-pétrole. Passerelle.*

Confédération Suisse. 2017. "Un premier pas vers des flux financiers compatibles avec le climat." *Press Release.* https://www.admin.ch/gov/fr/accueil/documentation/communiques.msg-id-68482.html.

Conseil Fédéral. 2015. *Perspectives 2030. Opportunités et dangers pour la Confédération.* Bern: Chancellerie de la Confédération suisse.

ConstruForce Canada. 2017. *Tendances mondiales: marchés du travail de la construction émergents.* Ottawa: ConstruForce Canada.

Contal, Marie-Hélène, ed. 2014. *Réenchanter le Monde. L'architecture et la ville face aux grandes transitions.* Paris: Alternatives.

Corcuff, Marie-Pascale. 2009. "L'architecture est aussi un art du temps." *Espaces-Temps.net* 09/11/2009. https://www.espacestemps.net/articles/architecture-est-aussi-un-art-du-temps/.

Cuchí, Albert, Joaquim Arcas-Abella, Marina Casals-Tres, and Gala Fombella. 2014. "Building a Common Home. Building Sector. A Global Vision Report." *World SB14 Barcelona Conference.* Barcelona, cuch. http://wsb-14barcelona.org/downloads/global-vision-report.pdf.

D

Daffara, Phillip. 2011. "Alternative City Futures." *Futures* 43 (7): 639–41. doi:10.1016/j.futures.2011.05.004.

Dalkey, Norman C. 1968. "Predicting the Future." *National Conference on Fluid Power, Chicago (Working Paper).* The RAND Corporation. https://www.rand.org/pubs/papers/P3948.html.

Daniels, Klaus. 1998. *Low-Tech, Light-Tech, High-Tech: Building in the Information Age.* Basel: Birkhauser Verlag AG.

Däpp, Walter. 2012. "Auch einsame Wölfe brauchen ein Rudel. Wie die Architekten." In *Bauart, Mehr Als Architektur, Booklet #006 (Werte).* Bern: Stämpfli.

Datar. 2010. "Territoires 2040, aménager le changement." *Revue d'Études et de Prospective* 1 (2e semestre): 103.

Désauney, Cécile, and François De Jouvenel. 2018. "Comment vivrons-nous en 2050? Synthèse des scénarios du rapport Vigie 2018 de Futuribles International." *Futuribles* 427: 5–25.

Devlieger, Lionel, and Maarten Gielen. 2014. *Behind the Green Door (the Book). A Critical Look at Sustainable Architecture through 600 Objects.* Edited by Lionel Devlieger. Oslo: Oslo Architecture Triennale.

Ducret, Raphaëlle. 2006. "Les raisons d'une démarche de prospective appliquée au territoire national." *Territoires 2040,* 51–56.

E

Emelianoff, Cyria, Elsa Mor, Michelle Dobre, Maxime Cordellier, and Carine Barbier. 2012. "Modes de vie et empreinte carbone. Prospective des modes de vie en France et empreinte carbone." *Cahiers du Club d'ingénierie Prospective Energie et Environnement (CLIP)* 21. Paris: 39–125.

Emerging Technology from the arXiv. 2017. "Global Urban Footprint Revealed in Unprecedented Resolution." *MIT Technology Review.* https://www-technology-review-com.cdn.ampproject.org/c/s/www.technology-review.com/s/608156/global-urban-footprint-revealed-in-unprecedented-resolution/amp/.

European Climate Foundation. 2010. "Roadmap 2050. A Practical Guide to a Prosperous, Low-Carbon Europe." *Policy* Volume 1 - (April): 1–9. doi:10.2833/10759.

F

Facundo, Alvaredo, Lucas Chancel, Thomas Piketty, Emmanuel Saez, and Gabriel Zucman, eds. 2018. *World Inequality Report 2018*. World Inequality Lab.

Favrat, Daniel. 2015. "Les 5 flops et les 5 tops de la transition énergétique." *L'Hebdo*.

Frick, Karin, and Christian Rauch. 2014. "Und nun: die Zukunft." *GDI IMPULS*, no. 2.

Futuribles. 2018. *Comment vivrons-nous? 20 questions pour 2050. Rapport Vigie 2018*. Paris: Futuribles international.

G

Gauzin-Müller, Dominique. 2002. *Sustainable Architecture and Urbanism*. Basel: Birkhäuser.

Gauzin-Müller, Dominique. 2006. *Sustainable Living: 25 International Examples*. Basel: Birkhäuser.

GCP Global, and Oxford Economics. 2015. *Global Construction 2030. A Global Forecast for the Construction Industry to 2030*.

Geyer, Roland, Jenna R. Jambeck, and Kara Lavender Law. 2017. "Production, Use, and Fate of All Plastics Ever Made." *Science Advances* 3 (7): e1700782. doi:10.1126/sciadv.1700782.

Ghyoot, Michaël, Lionel Devlieger, Lionel Billet, and André Warnier. 2018. *Déconstruction et réemploi. Comment faire circuler les éléments de construction*. Lausanne: Presses polytechniques et universitaires romandes.

Gidley, Jennifer M. 2016. "Understanding the Breadth of Futures Studies through a Dialogue with Climate Change." *World Futures Review* 8 (1): 24–38. doi:10.1177/1946756715627369.

Gidley, Jennifer M. 2017. *The Future: A Very Short Introduction*. Very Short. Oxford: Oxford University Press.

Global Chance. 2013. *Des questions qui fâchent. Contribution au débat national sur la transition énergétique*. Les Cahiers de Global Chance. Vol. 33.

Global Footprint Network. 2017a. "How Switzerland Made History with Green Economy Vote." Accessed September 25. http://www.footprintnetwork.org/2016/09/26/switzerland-made-history-green-economy-vote/.

Global Footprint Network. 2017b. "Watch Out, Dear Switzerland!" Accessed September 25. http://www.achtung-schweiz.org/en/.

Gontier, Pascal. 2017. "Sustainabilty as Integral Part of the Art of Building." *ArchiSTORM* Hors Série (July-August): 10–15.

Gontier, Pascal. 2018. *Home: l'habitat ouvert et sur mesure*. Paris: Museo éditions.

H

Hansen, James, Makiko Sato, Pushker Kharecha, David Beerling, Valerie Masson-Delmotte, Mark Pagani, Maureen Raymo, Dana L. Royer, and James C. Zachos. 2008. "Target Atmospheric CO_2: Where Should Humanity Aim?" *The Open Atmospheric Scientific Journal* 2: 217–31.

Harvey, L. D. Danny. 2009. "Reducing Energy Use in the Buildings Sector: Measures, Costs, and Examples." *Energy Efficiency* 2 (2): 139–63. doi:10.1007/s12053-009-9041-2.

Hawksworth, John, and Danny Chan. 2015. *The World in 2050: Will the Shift in Global Economic Power Continue?* https://www.pwc.com/gx/en/issues/the-economy/assets/world-in-2050-february-2015.pdf.

Heinrich von Thünen, Johann. 1966. *Der Isolierte Staat in Beziehung Auf Landwirtschaft und Nationalökonomie. Neu Herausgegeben*. Darmstadt: Wissenschaftliche Buchgesellschaft.

Helmer-Hirschberg, Olaf. 1967. "Analysis of the Future: The Delphi Method." *Rivista Italiana di Amministrazione Industriale (Working Paper)*. The RAND Corporation. https://www.rand.org/pubs/papers/P3558.html.

Hirabayashi, Yukiko, Roobavannan Mahendran, Sujan Koirala, Lisako Konoshima, Dai Yamazaki, Satoshi Watanabe, Hyungjun Kim, and Shinjiro Kanae. 2013. "Global Flood Risk under Climate Change." *Nature Climate Change* 3: 816–21. http://dx.doi.org/10.1038/nclimate1911.

Hurtt, George C., Louise Parsons Chini, Steve Frolking, R. A. Betts, Johannes Fedema, G. Fischer, Justin P. Fisk, et al. 2011. "Harmonization of Land-Use Scenarios for the Period 1500–2100: 600 Years of Global Gridded Annual Land-Use Transitions, Wood Harvest, and Resulting Secondary Lands." *Climatic Change*, 109–17. doi:10.1007/s10584-011-0153-2.

I

Ingraham, Christopher. 2017. "The Difference between Night and Day Is Disappearing, Scientists Warn." *The Washington Post*. http://wapo.st/2A48YEd?tid=ss_mail&utm_term=.72f131446408.

International Energy Agency. 2013. *Transition to Sustainable Buildings. Strategies and Opportunities to 2050*. Paris: OECD/IEA.

International Energy Agency. 2015. *Renewable Energy. Medium-Term Market Report 2015. Market Analysis and Forecasts to 2020*. Paris: IEA.

International Energy Agency. 2018. *Renewables 2018. Market Analysis and Forecast from 2018 to 2023*. Paris: IEA.

IPCC. 1992. *Climate Change: The IPCC 1990 and 1992 Assessments*. Geneva: WHO, UNEP.

IPCC. 2001. *Climate Change 2001: Impacts, Adaptation, and Vulnerability*. Edited by James McCarthy, Osvaldo Canziani, Neil Leary, David Dokken, and Kasey White. Cambridge: Cambridge University Press.

IPCC. 2014. *Climate Change 2014: Synthesis Report*. Edited by Rajendra K Pachauri and Leo Meyer. *Contribution of Working Groups I, II and III to the Fifth Assessment Report of the Intergovernmental Panel on Climate Change*. Geneva: IPCC.

IPCC. 2018. "Summary for Policy Makers." In *Global Warming of 1.5°C. An IPCC Special Report on the Impacts of Global Warming of 1.5°C above Pre-Industrial Levels and Related Global Greenhouse Gas Emission Pathways, in the Context of Strengthening the Global Response to the Threat of Climate Change*, edited by Valerie Masson-Delmotte, Panmao Zhai, Hans-Otto Pörtner, Debra Roberts, James Skea, Priyadarshi Shukla, Anna Pirani, et al., 32. Geneva: World Meteorological Organization.

K

Khan, Ahmed, and Karen Allacker. 2015. *Architecture and Sustainability: Critical Perspectives for Integrated Design*. Leuven: Acco.

King Sturge, RICS Foundation, The University of Salford, and The Futures Academy. 2010. *Built Environment Foresight 2030 : The Sustainable Development Imperative*.

Klein Goldewijk, Kees, Arthur Beusen, Gerard Van Drecht, and Martine De Vos. 2011. "The HYDE 3.1 Spatially Explicit Database of Human-Induced Global Land-Use Change over the Past 12 000 Years." *Global Ecology and Biogeography* 20 (1): 73–86. doi:10.1111/j.1466-8238.2010.00587.x.

L

Labelle, Alain. 2017. "Changements climatiques: 7 défis pour l'humanité." *Radio Canada*. http://ici.radio-canada.ca/nouvelle/1067326/changements-climatiques-defis-humanite-villes-submergees-ouragan-secheresse-pollution-refugie-famine.

Lechner, Norbert. 2008. *Heating, Cooling, Lighting: Sustainable Methods for Architects*. Hoboken: John Wiley & Sons.

Lévy, Jacques, and Thierry Paquot. 2016. *Ville en partage – Urbanisme et urbanistes en 2030*. Paris: Conseil Français des Urbanistes.

Lewino, Frédéric. 2017. "Depuis 1950, l'Homme a produit un Himalaya de plastique." *Le Point*. http://www.lepoint.fr/environnement/depuis-1950-l-homme-a-produit-un-himalaya-de-plastique-19-07-2017-2144386_1927.php.

Li, Minqi. 2017. *World Energy 2017-2050: Annual Report*. Department of Economics, University of Utah.

Lufkin, Sophie, Emmanuel Rey, and Suren Erkman. 2016. *Strategies for Symbiotic Urban Neighbourhoods. Towards Local Energy Self-Sufficiency*. New York: Springer.

M

MacKay, David. 2009. *Sustainable Energy – without the Hot Air*. Cambridge: UIT Cambridge.

Maresca, Bruno. 2014. "Sur le chemin de la sobriété énergétique. Engager les Français au-delà des écogestes." *CREDOC – Consommation et*

Meadows, Dennis, Jørgen Randers, and Donella H. Meadows. 2004. *The Limits to Growth – The 30-Years Update*. London: Earthscan.

Meadows, Donella H., Dennis Meadows, Jørgen Randers, and William W. Behrens III. 1972. *The Limits to Growth: A Report for the Club of Rome's Project on the Predicament of Mankind*. New York: Universe Books.

Ménard, Raphaël. 2011. "Dense Cities in 2050 : The Energy Option?" *ECEEE 2011 Summer Study. Energy Efficiency First: The Foundation of a Low-Carbon Society*, 873–84.

Metcalfe, John. 2017. "The World's Soaring CO_2 Levels Visualized as Skyscrapers." https://www.citylab.com/environment/2017/09/the-worlds-skyrocketing-co2-levels-visualized-as-skyscrapers/540255/.

N

Nehring, Richard. 2009. "Traversing the Mountaintop: World Fossil Fuel Production to 2050." *Philosophical Transactions of the Royal Society B: Biological Sciences* 364 (1532): 3067–79. doi:10.1098/rstb.2009.0170.

Newman, Peter, and Jeffrey Kenworthy. 1999. *Sustainability and Cities. Overcoming Automobile Dependence*. Washington: Island Press.

O

OECD. 2012. *OECD Environmental Outlook to 2050*. Paris: OECD Publishing. https://dx.doi.org/10.1787/9789264122246-en.

Office Fédéral de l'Energie (OFEN). 2011. "Réseaux énergétiques. L'alpha et l'oméga de l'approvisionnement énergétique." *Energeia. Bulletin de l'Office Fédéral de l'Energie OFEN*.

Office Fédéral de l'Environnement (OFEV). 2015. *Adaptation aux changements climatiques. Connaissance de l'environnement*. Vol. 18. doi:10.1051/nss/2010034.

Office Fédéral de Météorologie et de Climatologie (MétéoSuisse). 2017. "Quand l'extrême devient la normale." http://www.meteosuisse.admin.ch/home.subpage.html/fr/data/blogs/2017/11/das-extreme-wird-normal.html.

Owen, Bethan, David S. Lee, and Ling Lim. 2010. "Flying into the Future: Aviation Emissions Scenarios to 2050." *Environmental Science and Technology* 44 (7): 2255–60. doi:10.1021/es902530z.

P

Pfammatter, Ulrich. 2008. *Building the Future: Building Technology and Cultural History from the Industrial Revolution Until Today*. Munich: Prestel Publishing.

Pfammatter, Ulrich. 2014. *World Atlas of Sustainable Architecture: Building for a Changing Culture and Climate*. Berlin: DOM Publishers.

Picon, Antoine. 2010. *Digital Culture in Architecture. An Introduction for the Design Professions*. Basel: Birkhäuser.

Picon, Antoine. 2013. *Smart Cities. Théorie et critique d'un idéal auto-réalisateur*. Collection Actualités. Paris: Editions B2.

Picon, Antoine. 2015. *Smart Cities: A Spatialised Intelligence*. Hoboken (New Jersey): John Wiley & Sons.

Picon, Antoine. 2018. *La Matérialité de L'architecture*. Marseille: Parenthèses.

Plumer, Brad, and Nadja Popovich. 2017. "Here's How Far the World Is From Meeting its Climate Goals." *The New York Times*. https://nyti.ms/2hLm80R.

Prost, Robert. 1992. *Conception architecturale. Une investigation méthodologique*. Paris: L'Harmattan.

R

Ratcliffe, John, and Ela Krawczyk. 2011. "Imagineering City Futures: The Use of Prospective through Scenarios in Urban Planning." *Futures* 43 (7): 642–53. doi:10.1016/j.futures.2011.05.005.

Revedin, Jana, and Marie-Hélène Contal. 2018. *Sustainable Design 6: Vers une nouvelle éthique pour l'architecture et la ville / Towards a New Ethics for Architecture and the City*. Paris: Alternatives.

Rey, Emmanuel. 2013. "Vers une architecture durable." In *GREEN DENSITY*, 181–84. Lausanne: Presses polytechniques et universitaires romandes.

Rey, Emmanuel. 2015. *From Spatial Development to Detail*. Notatio. Lucerne: Quart.

Rey, Emmanuel, and Sophie Lufkin. 2016. "GREEN DENSITY. A Transdisciplinary Research and Teaching Project for the Design of Sustainable Neighbourhoods." *Gaia-Ecological Perspectives for Science and Society* 25 (3): 185–90. doi:10.14512/gaia.25.3.10.

Ripple, William J., Christopher Wolf, Thomas M. Newsome, Mauro Galetti, Mohammed Alamgir, Eileen Crist, Mahmoud I. Mahmoud, and William F. Laurance. 2017. "World Scientists' Warning to Humanity: A Second Notice." *BioScience* 67 (12): 1026–28. doi:10.1093/biosci/bix125.

Rogers, Chris, Rachel Lombardi, Joanne Leach, and Rachel Cooper. 2012. "The Urban Futures Methodology Applied to Urban Regeneration." *Proceedings of the Institution of Civil Engineers, Engineering Sustainability* 165 (ES1): 5–20. doi:10.1680/ensu.2012.165.1.5.

Rother, Natanael. 2017. "Avenir Suisse – Comment nous portons-nous?" *Avenir Suisse*. https://www.avenir-suisse.ch/fr/microsite/repartition/.

Roush, Wade, ed. 2018. *Twelve Tomorrows*. Cambridge: MIT Press.

Rousseau, Nicolas. 2017. "Génération 2050: à la poursuite des modes de vie de demain." *Acteurs de L'économie – La Tribune*. https://m.usbeketrica.com/article/generation-2050-a-la-poursuite-des-modes-de-vie-de-demain.

RTS Info. 2017. "La Suisse a officiellement adhéré à l'accord de Paris sur le climat." https://www.rts.ch/info/sciences-tech/8979011-la-suisse-a-officiellement-adhere-a-l-accord-de-paris-sur-le-climat.html.

Ruby, Ilka, Andreas Ruby, and Nathalie Janson, eds. 2014. *The Economy of Sustainable Construction*. Berlin: Ruby Press.

S

Schrag, Daniel. 2013. "Extreme Weather and Climate Change: An Interview with Harvard Climate Scientists." *Environment@Harvard - Newsletter of the Center for the Environment* 5 (1): 18–21.

Schröpfer, Thomas. 2012. *Ecological Urban Architecture: Qualitative Approaches to Sustainability*. Basel: Birkhäuser.

Schröpfer, Thomas. 2015. *Dense + Green: Innovative Building Types for Sustainable Urban Architecture*. Basel: Birkhäuser.

Schröpfer, Thomas, and Sacha Menz. 2018. *Dense and Green Building Typologies. Research, Policy and Practice Perspectives*. SpringerBriefs in Architectural Design and Technology. Berlin: Springer.

Serres, Michel. 2011. *Habiter*. Paris: Le Pommier.

Steffen, Will, Asa Persson, Lisa Deutsch, Jan Zalasiewicz, Mark Williams, Katherine Richardson, Carole Crumley, et al. 2011. "The Anthropocene: From Global Change to Planetary Stewardship." *Ambio* 40 (7): 739–61. doi:10.1007/s13280-011-0185-x.

Stojanovic, Milica, Petar Mitkovic, and Mihailo Mitkovic. 2014. "The Scenario Method in Urban Planning." *Facta Universitatis – Series: Architecture and Civil Engineering* 12 (1): 81–95. doi:10.2298/FUACE1401081S.

Sutton, Jane. 2013. "Four New Centres of Excellence for Sustainable Building Design Launched." http://www.raeng.org.uk/news/news-releases/2013/May/four-new-centres-of-excellence-for-sustainable-bui.

T

The Royal Academy of Engineering. 2010. *Engineering a Low Carbon Built Environment: The Discipline of Building Engineering Physics*. London: The Royal Academy of Engineering.

The Royal Academy of Engineering. 2012. *The Case for Centres of Excellence in Sustainable Building Design*. London: The Royal Academy of Engineering.

Thöma, Jakob, Claire Murray, Michael Hayne, and Klaus Hagedorn. 2017. *Eclairage sur la cohérence climatique du portefeuille des assureurs et caisses de pensions suisses*. New York, London, Paris, Berlin: 2°Investing Initiative, PACTA.

Turner, Graham. 2014. "Is Global Collapse Imminent?" *Melbourne Sustainable Society Institute Research Paper* 4 (4). Melbourne Sustainable Society Institute, The University of Melbourne.

U

U.S. Energy Information Administration (EIA). 2016. *Energy and Air Pollution. World Energy Outlook Special Report*. https://www.iea.org/publications/freepublications/publication/WorldEnergyOutlookSpecialReport2016EnergyandAirPollution.pdf.

U.S. Energy Information Administration (EIA). 2017. *Annual Energy Outlook 2017 with Projections to 2050*. https://www.eia.gov/outlooks/aeo/pdf/0383(2017).pdf.

Union of Concerned Scientists. 2013. "Causes of Sea Level Rise: What the Science Tells Us." *Fact Sheet*. www.ucsusa.org/sealevelrisescience.

United Nations. 1992. *Agenda 21*. Rio de Janeiro Earth Summit.

United Nations. 2015a. *Paris Agreement*. Paris. https://ec.europa.eu/clima/policies/international/negotiations/paris_en.

United Nations. 2015b. *Resolution Adopted by the General Assembly on 25 September 2015*. http://www.un.org/ga/search/view_doc.asp?symbol=A/RES/70/1&Lang=E.

United Nations. 2015c. *Transforming Our World: The 2030 Agenda for Sustainable Development. Resolution Adopted by the General Assembly on 25 September 2015*. New York: United Nations.

United Nations Department of Economic and Social Affairs. 2016. *The World's Cities in 2016*. New York: United Nations.

United Nations Department of Economic and Social Affairs. 2017. *World Population Prospects: The 2017 Revision*. New York: United Nations. https://esa.un.org/unpd/wpp/Download/Standard/Population/.

United Nations, and WCED. 1987. *Our Common Future (Brundtland Report)*.

Ürge-Vorsatz, Diana, Luisa F. Cabeza, Susana Serrano, Camila Barreneche, and Ksenia Petrichenko. 2015. "Heating and Cooling Energy Trends and Drivers in Buildings." *Renewable and Sustainable Energy Reviews* 41: 85–98. doi:10.1016/j.rser.2014.08.039.

V

Von Weizsacker, Ernst. 1998. *Factor Four: Doubling Wealth, Halving Resource Use – A Report to the Club of Rome*. Abingdon-on-Thames: Routledge.

Vuille, François, Daniel Favrat, and Suren Erkman. 2015. *Les enjeux de la transition énergétique suisse*. Lausanne: Presses polytechniques et universitaires romandes.

W

Winston, Ana. 2010. "2050 : Where Will Architecture Be in 40 Years ?" *Bdonline –* (March): 1–8.

World Bank. 2017. *Atlas of Sustainable Development Goals 2017 : World Development Indicators*. Washington DC: World Bank. doi:10.1596/978-1-4648-1080-0.

World Bank. 2018. *Atlas of Sustainable Development Goals 2018 : World Development Indicators*. Washington DC: World Bank. doi:10.1596/978-1-4648-1250-7.

WWF. 2008. *Living Planet Report 2008*. Edited by Chris Hails, Sarah Humphrey, Jonathan Loh, and Steven Goldfinger. Gland: WWF.

WWF. 2016. *Living Planet Report 2016. Risk and Resilience in a New Era*. Edited by Natasja Oerlemans, Holly Strand, Annemarie Winkelhagen, Mike Barrett, and Monique Grooten. Gland: WWF.

WWF. 2018. *Living Planet Report 2018. Aiming Higher*. Edited by Monique Grooten and Rosamunde Almond. Gland: WWF.

Illustration credits

Pages 1–8 Jeremy Ayer, "BlueFactory", (September 2018).

Introduction
A, B, C   United Nations Department of Economic and Social Affairs. 2017. *World Population Prospects: The 2017 Revision*. New York: United Nations.
D   WWF. 2008. *Living Planet Report 2008*. Edited by Chris Hails, Sarah Humphrey, Jonathan Loh, and Steven Goldfinger. Gland: WWF.
E   Li, Minqi. 2017. *World Energy 2017-2050: Annual Report*. Department of Economics, University of Utah.
F   IPCC. 2013. "Annex II: Climate System Scenario Tables." In *Climate Change 2013: The Physical Science Basis. Contribution of Working Group I to the Fifth Assessment Report of the Intergovernmental Panel on Climate Change*, edited by Michael Prather, Gregory Flato, Pierre Friedlingstein, Christopher Jones, Jean-François Lamarque, Hong Liao, and Philip Rasch. Cambridge and New York: Cambridge University Press.

Pages 23–34   graphic-recording.cool (Johanna Benz & Tiziana Beck), 2018.

Tatiana Bilbao
A   United Nations Department of Economic and Social Affairs. 2017. *World Population Prospects: The 2017 Revision*. New York: United Nations.
B   Jaime Navarro Photographer (image), Tatiana Bilbao Estudio (drawings).
C   Rory Gardiner (image top), Rodolfo Díaz Cervantes (image bottom), Tatiana Bilbao Estudio (drawings).
D   Tom Harris.
E   Iwan Baan (images), Tatiana Bilbao Estudio (drawings).

Paula Cadima
A   World Health Organization. 2018. *World Health Statistics 2018. Monitoring Health for the Sustainable Development Goals*. Geneva: World Health Organization.
B   Pascale Sury.
C   Pastore, Luisa. 2017. *Looking at Minergie Buildings from the User's Perspective. Insights from a Post-Occupancy Evaluation and a Façade Design Analysis*.

IDEAS Lunch. Lausanne: EPFL.
D   Olivier Wavre.

Lionel Devlieger
A   Eric Mairiaux.
B   Rotor.
C   Rotor (images top), Klaas Verdru (image bottom).
D   Eric Mairiaux.

Herbert Girardet
A   Ilimelgo.
B   Ashley Cooper (image), Arup (drawing).
C   David Clarke.

Alistair Guthrie
A   Simon Kennedy.
B   Angus Martin.
C, D   Michel Denancé.
E   Daniel Imade, Arup
F   Ballif, Christophe, Laure-Emmanuelle Perret-Aebi, Sophie Lufkin, and Emmanuel Rey. 2018. "Integrated Thinking for Photovoltaics in Buildings." *Nature Energy* 3: 438–42.

Kengo Kuma
A   Eiichi Kano (images), Kengo Kuma & Associates (drawing).
B   Michel Denancé (images), Kengo Kuma & Associates (drawing).
C   Takumi Ota (image), Kengo Kuma & Associates (drawings).
D   Daici Ano (images), Kengo Kuma & Associates (drawing).

Ali Malkawi
A   Snøhetta/Plompmozes.
B   Snøhetta.

Edward Ng
A   World Bank. 2013. *The World Bank Annual Report 2013*. Washington DC: World Bank. doi:10.1596/978-0-8213-9937-8.
B   Federal Reserve Economic Data (FRED) and Scripps Institution of Oceanography (SIO).
C   One University One Village, The Chinese University of Hong Kong.

Susan Parnell
A   Central Intelligence Agency (CIA). 2016. *The World Factbook 2016–2017*. Washington DC: CIA.
B   United Nations Department of Economic and Social Affairs. 2017. *World Population Prospects: The 2017 Revision*. New York: United Nations. https://esa.un.org/unpd/wpp/Download/Standard/Population/.
C   World Bank. 2017. *Atlas of Sustainable Development Goals 2017 : World Development Indicators*. Washington DC: World Bank. doi:10.1596/978-1-4648-1080-0.
D   WWF. 2016. *Living Planet Report 2016. Risk and Resilience in a New Era*. Edited by Natasja Oerlemans, Holly Strand, Annemarie Winkelhagen, Mike Barrett, and Monique Grooten. Gland: WWF.

Antoine Picon
A   World Bank. 2011. *World Development Report 2011*. Washington DC: World Bank.
B   Andrew, Robbie M. 2018. "Global CO_2 Emissions from Cement Production." *Earth System Science Data* 10: 195–217.

Carlo Ratti
A   U.S. Energy Information Administration (EIA). 2012. *Annual Energy Outlook 2012. With Projections to 2035*.
B   i-scoop.
C   CRA-Carlo Ratti Associati.
D, E   MIT Senseable City Lab.
F   David Pike (images), CRA-Carlo Ratti Associati (drawings).

Koen Steemers
A   International Energy Agency. 2013. *Transition to Sustainable Buildings. Strategies and Opportunities to 2050*. Paris: OECD/IEA.
B   European Parliament. 2016. *Boosting Building Renovation: What Potential and Value for Europe?* Brussels: European Parliament.
C   Image courtesy of Assemble.

Pages 209–215   Jeremy Ayer, "BlueFactory", (September 2018).

Authors

Marilyne Andersen holds an MSc in Physics and a PhD in Building Physics from the École polytechnique fédérale de Lausanne (EPFL), where she is a professor of sustainable construction technologies and head of the Laboratory of Integrated Performance in Design (LIPID). Her research at LIPID focuses on the integration of building performance in design, with an emphasis on daylighting and themes such as health, perception, comfort and energy. She was Dean of the School of Architecture, Civil and Environmental Engineering (ENAC) at EPFL from 2013 to 2018 and is the Academic Director of the *smart living lab*. Before joining EPFL as faculty member, she was a Visiting Scholar at the Lawrence Berkeley National Laboratory, and Assistant then Associate Professor at MIT (USA), where she founded the MIT Daylighting Lab in 2004. She is the author of over 100 refereed scientific papers, several of which have earned distinctions, and was the first laureate of The Award for Daylight Research in 2016. She was also the leader of and faculty advisor to the Swiss Team, which won the 2017 US Solar Decathlon competition. She is co-founder of the start-up OCULIGHT dynamics, is a member of the Board of the LafargeHolcim Foundation for Sustainable Construction, an expert for Inno-Suisse and a Foundation Culture du Bâti (CUB) board member.

Emmanuel Rey earned a degree in architecture at École polytechnique fédérale de Lausanne (EPFL), followed by a European postgraduate diploma in architecture and sustainable development (1999) and a PhD from the Université catholique de Louvain (2006). His doctoral thesis was awarded the European Gustave Magnel Prize in 2009. Since 2000, he has worked at Bauart, an architectural and urban design firm based in Bern, Neuchâtel and Zurich, and has been a partner there since 2004. Through his work, he is involved in a wide variety of projects, competitions and achievements that have been published, exhibited and/or awarded on several occasions. He has also been professor of architecture and sustainable construction technologies at EPFL, where he founded the Laboratory of Architecture and Sustainable Technologies (LAST), since 2010. His contributions focus on the transcription of sustainability principles into architectural design, from the neighbourhood scale to construction components. He has been involved in the conceptual development of the *smart living lab* from its inception, and was Chair of the Smart Living Building Scientific Committee from 2014 to 2016. In 2015, he received an award from the Swiss Academies of Arts and Sciences and the swiss-academies award for transdisciplinary research (td-award).

Sophie Lufkin earned a degree in architecture from the École polytechnique fédérale de Lausanne (EPFL) in 2005. She is also the author of a doctoral thesis on the potential for densification of disused railway areas (EPFL, 2010). After international experience at LAR-Fernando Romero (Mexico City), she is currently working as a researcher and lecturer at the EPFL's Laboratory of Architecture and Sustainable Technologies (LAST), led by Professor Emmanuel Rey. Her research is part of the global move towards increased sustainability in the built environment, particularly at the neighbourhood scale.

Emilie Nault completed a PhD at the Laboratory of Integrated Performance in Design (LIPID) at the École polytechnique fédérale de Lausanne (EPFL) in 2016. She carried on there as a postdoctoral researcher, sharing her time between LIPID and the Laboratory of Architecture and Sustainable Technologies (LAST) before joining the "Building2050" group (*smart living lab*, EPFL-Fribourg) as a scientific collaborator in 2018. Her research and development activities focus on methods and tools to support environmental performance-driven decision-making in urban planning and design.

Stakeholders

Research team

Vision 2050 Research Group

Supervision
Prof. Emmanuel Rey, Head of Laboratory of Architecture and Sustainable Technologies (LAST)
Principal investigator
Dr. Sophie Lufkin, Scientific Collaborator, Laboratory of Architecture and Sustainable Technologies (LAST)
Members
Prof. Marilyne Andersen, Academic Director of the *smart living lab*, Head of Laboratory of Integrated Performance in Design (LIPID) and Building2050 Group
Dr. Emilie Nault, Scientific Collaborator, Laboratory of Integrated Performance in Design (LIPID) and Building2050 Group

Committees

Joint Steering Committee

Canton of Fribourg
Olivier Curty, State Councillor, Co-Chair of the Joint Steering Committee
Jean-Pierre Siggen, State Councillor
Jean-Luc Mossier, Managing Director of the Canton of Fribourg Development Agency
École polytechnique fédérale de Lausanne
Etienne Marclay, Vice President for Human Resources & Operations EPFL, Co-Chair of the Joint Steering Committee
Andreas Mortensen, Vice President for Research EPFL
Marc Gruber, Vice President for Innovation EPFL
Marilyne Andersen, Dean of School of Architecture, Civil and Environmental Engineering EPFL
School of Engineering and Architecture of Fribourg
Jean-Nicolas Aebischer, Director of School of Engineering and Architecture of Fribourg
University of Fribourg
Astrid Epiney, Rector University of Fribourg

Operational Committee

Canton of Fribourg
Olivier Allaman, Director Company Foundation and Innovation at the Canton of Fribourg Development Agency
École polytechnique fédérale de Lausanne
Prof. Corentin Fivet, Head of Structural Xploration Lab (SXL)
School of Engineering and Architecture of Fribourg
Prof. Jean-Philippe Bacher, Co-Head of ENERGY Institute, *smart living lab* HEIA-FR Manager, Technology transfer manager
University of Fribourg (UNIFR)
Prof. Stephanie Teufel, Head of international institute of management in technology
smart living lab
Anne-Claude Cosandey, Director of Operations EPFL Fribourg and *smart living lab*
Former members (2014–2016)
Beat Vonlanthen, former State Councillor, Co-Chair of the Joint Steering Committee
Philippe Gillet, former Vice President for Academic Affairs EPFL, Co-Chair of the Joint Steering Committee
Adrienne Corboud, former Vice President for Innovation EPFL
André Schneider, former Vice President for Infrastructure EPFL

Commissions

Scientific Commission
smart living lab

Chair
Prof. Marilyne Andersen, Academic Director of the *smart living lab*, Head of Laboratory of Integrated Performance in Design (LIPID) and of Building2050 Group

Members
École polytechnique fédérale de Lausanne
Dr. Anne-Claude Cosandey, Director of Operations EPFL Fribourg and *smart living lab*
Prof. Corentin Fivet, Head of Structural Xploration Lab (SXL)
Thomas Jusselme, Building2050 Group, Project Manager
Prof. Dolaana Khovalyg, Head of Thermal Engineering for Built Environment Lab (TEBEL)
Prof. Dusan Licina, Head of Human-Oriented Built Environment Lab (HOBEL)
Prof. Paolo Tombesi, Head of Laboratory of Construction and Architecture (FAR)
School of Engineering and Architecture of Fribourg
Prof. Elena-Lavinia Niederhauser, Co-Head of ENERGY Institute
Prof. Jean-Philippe Bacher, Co-Head of ENERGY Institute / *smart living lab* HEIA-FR Manager
Prof. Florinel Radu, Head of TRANSFORM Institute
Prof. Daia Zwicky, Head of iTEC Institute
University of Fribourg
Prof. Martin Beyeler, Institute for Swiss and international construction law
Prof. Denis Lalanne, Head of Human-IST Research Center
Prof. Stephanie Teufel, Head of international institute of management in technology

Scientific Commission
Smart Living Building (2014–2016)

Chair
Prof. Emmanuel Rey, Head of Laboratory of Architecture and Sustainable Technologies (LAST)

Co-chair
Prof. Marilyne Andersen, Academic Director of the *smart living lab*, Head of Laboratory of Integrated Performance in Design (LIPID) and of Building2050 Group

Members
École polytechnique fédérale de Lausanne
Dr. Anne-Claude Cosandey, Director of Operations EPFL Fribourg and *smart living lab*
Prof. Corentin Fivet, Head of Structural Xploration Lab (SXL), Professor
Prof. Thomas Keller, Head of Composite Construction Laboratory (CCLAB)
Prof. Jean-Louis Scartezzini, Head of Solar Energy and Building Physics Laboratory (LESO-PB)
Prof. Paolo Tombesi, Head of Laboratory of Construction and Architecture (FAR)
School of Engineering and Architecture of Fribourg
Prof. Jean-Philippe Bacher, Co-Head of ENERGY Institute / *smart living lab* HEIA-FR Manager
Prof. Jacques Bersier, Head of applied research and development
Prof. Elena-Lavinia Niederhauser, Co-Head of ENERGY Institute
Prof. Florinel Radu, Head of TRANSFORM Institute
Prof. Daia Zwicky, Head of iTEC Institute
University of Fribourg
Prof. Martin Beyeler, Institute for Swiss and international construction law
Prof. Denis Lalanne, Head of Human-IST Research Center
Dr. Arnold Rusch, Privatdozent
Prof. Stephanie Teufel, Head of international institute of management in technology
Prof. Jean-Baptiste Zufferey, Administrative Law Professor
Swiss Federal Laboratories for Materials Science and Technology (EMPA)
Peter Richner, Deputy Director
External consultant
Noël Schneider

Workshops

Design process workshop
Fribourg, March 7–8, 2017

Chair
Marilyne Andersen, Academic Director of the *smart living lab*, Head of Laboratory of Integrated Performance in Design (LIPID) and of Building2050 Group
Anne-Claude Cosandey, Director of Operations EPFL Fribourg and *smart living lab*

Organisation
Elvio Alloi, DII Constructions EPFL
Delphine Blauer, DII Constructions EPFL
Florinel Radu, TRANSFORM HEIA-FR
Paolo Tombesi, FAR EPFL

Coordination
Vanda Costa Grisel, Building2050 Group EPFL

Participants
Jean-Philippe Bacher, ENERGY HEIA-FR
Martin Beyeler, Institute for Swiss and International Construction Law UNIFR
Jonas Brulhart, DII Exploitation EPFL
Corentin Fivet, SXL EPFL
Thomas Jusselme, Building2050 Group EPFL
Denis Lalanne, HUMAN-IST UNIFR
Olivier Monney, HEIA-FR
Jean-Luc Mossier, Canton of Fribourg Development Agency
Emmanuel Rey, LAST EPFL
Kirstin Stadelmann, iimt UNIFR
Stephanie Teufel, iimt UNIFR
Barbara Tirone, ENAC-DO EPFL
Didier Vuarnoz, Building2050 Group EPFL

Scientific workshop
Gruyeres, October 5–6, 2016

Chair
Marilyne Andersen, Academic Director of the *smart living lab*, Head of Laboratory of Integrated Performance in Design (LIPID) and of Building2050 Group EPFL

Organisation
Thomas Jusselme, Project Manager Building2050 Group EPFL

Coordination
Vanda Costa Grisel, Scientific Collaborator Building2050 Group EPFL

Participants
Karen Allacker, KU Leuven
Sibylla Amstutz, Lucerne University of Applied Sciences and Arts
Annette Aumann, City of Zürich
Jean-Philippe Bacher, ENERGY HEIA-FR
Stéphanie Bender, 2b architectes
Arianna Brambilla, Building2050 Group EPFL
Hanspeter Bürgi, Bürgi & Shärer
Anne-Claude Cosandey, *smart living lab*
Enrico Costanza, UCL Interaction Center, University College London
Stefano Cozza, Building2050 Group EPFL
François Esquivié, TRANSFORM HEIA-FR
Stéphane Gerbex, Alpiq
John Haymaker, Perkins & Will
Per Heiselberg, Faculty of Engineering and Science Aalborg University
Endrit Hoxha, Building2050 Group EPFL
Niels Jungbluth, ESU-service
Denis Lalanne, Human-IST UNIFR
Benson Lau, University of Westminster School of Architecture
Cédric Liardet, Building2050 Group EPFL
Heinrich Manz, Lucerne University of Applied Sciences and Arts
Emanuele Naboni, The Royal Danish Academy of Fine Arts
Steffi Neubert, Emmer Pfenninger Partner
Wim Pullen, Center for People and Buildings Delft
Florinel Radu, TRANSFORM HEIA-FR
Emmanuel Rey, LAST EPFL
Josep Ricart, H arquitectes
Philip Ross, Unwork
Igor Sartori, SINTEF
Jean-Louis Scartezzini, LESO-PB EPFL
Philippe Stolz, Treeze
Didier Vuarnoz, Building2050 Group EPFL
Paul Wargocki, Department of Civil Engineering, Technical University of Denmark

Acknowledgements & Imprint

The editors would like to thank, first of all, the twelve experts who accepted the invitation with enthusiasm and contributed their valuable time to shed light on key challenges and opportunities for architectural design. They also express their gratitude to the members of the research team and the interviewees' assistants and collaborators as well as to swissnex Boston, in particular Felix Moesner, Jonas Brunschwig and Cécile Vulliemin, for their constructive communication and efficient exchanges throughout the editorial process.

The editors likewise extend their thanks to the scientists and colleagues who put their precious expertise at the service of refining the interview guide, in particular Emanuele Naboni, associate professor of sustainable and climatic design at the Institute of Architecture and Technology at The Royal Danish Academy of Fine Arts Schools of Architecture, Design and Conservation (KADK), and Dr. Luca Pattaroni, senior scientist at the Urban Sociology Laboratory (LASUR) at the EPFL. Our thanks also go to the different members of the Joint Steering Committee, the Operational Committee, the Scientific Commission of the *smart living lab* and the Scientific Commission of the Smart Living Building for their support during the development of this project.

The editors are grateful to everyone who made this book and its distribution possible: the designers Marco Walser and Marina Brugger, the photographer Jeremy Ayer, the infographist Barbara Hoffmann, the copy editor Jessica Strelec, the proofreader Emily Darrow, the printer Kösel and the publisher Park Books.

Last but not least, the editors' thanks also go to the Canton of Fribourg for its essential financial support and, more broadly, to the multiple stakeholders from the three Swiss universities—the School of Architecture, Civi and Environmental Engineering (ENAC) at the École polytechnique fédérale de Lausanne (EPFL), the School of Engineering and Architecture of Fribourg (HEIA-FR) and the University of Fribourg (UNIFR)—who have, directly or indirectly, contributed to this research and publication.

Design and typesetting
Elektrosmog, Zurich
Marco Walser and Marina Brugger

Graphic and editorial coordination
Sophie Lufkin, Lausanne

Photography
Photo reportage in Fribourg
Jeremy Ayer, Zurich / Fribourg

Illustrations & Cover image
graphicrecording.cool (Johanna Benz & Tiziana Beck, Leipzig / Paris)

Infography
Barbara Hoffmann, Leipzig / Zurich

Typeface
Alpha Grotesk
Simon Mager, Omnitype

Color separation
Color Library
www.colorlibrary.ch

Copy editing
Jessica Strelec, Valgorge

Proofreading
Emily Darrow, Brussels

Printing
Kösel GmbH & Co. KG, Altusried-Krugzell

Publisher
Park Books
Niederdorfstrasse 54
8001 Zurich
Switzerland
www.park-books.com

Park Books is being supported by the Federal Office of Culture with a general subsidy for the years 2016–2020.

All rights reserved; no part of this publication may be reproduced, stored in a retrieval system or transmitted in any form or by any means, electronic, mechanical, photocopying, recording, or otherwise, without the prior written consent of the editors and the publisher.

ISBN 978-3-03860-131-9